**"I didn't expect it t**

**"Fun to read**. There are a lot of relationship books which are either dry and boring or that belabor certain points over and over again; this is not one of those books."
                    - Elizabeth Trull on *Amazon.com*


**"…encouraging and Biblical advice that can powerfully impact your marriage."**
                    - Lisa Jacobson, *Club 31 Women*


**"Thought provoking.** We have a good marriage, but reading this has really opened my eyes to areas that I can improve in....and make our marriage even better."
                    - JamiB, *Homeschool Mama*


"I have always respected my husband, but this book is helping me demonstrate it in practical ways that bless him. **I have seen wonderful results in our marriage.** We are having more fun together, and I am experiencing the freedom and joy that come from honoring my husband. And as he feels my respect, he is more inclined to demonstrate love in ways that bless me. It's a win-win situation!"
                    - Texas Theresa on *Amazon.com*


**"I have been married 20 years and found it helpful."**
                    - CJ on *Amazon.com*

"**Great ideas** on how to show the most important man in my life how much I value him. Highly recommended."
      - Rebecca Clayton on *Amazon.com*

"...gracious, spirit-filled advice for all wives seeking to improve their marital relationship.... **Easy to read and definitely worth the time it takes to do so.**"
      - Patricia Day, *Climb Your Mountains*

"I found the book to offer a smooth, yet refined look into a valuable area of knowledge, so often limited or misguided by our society. Although its title seems simple, it is not simply a how-to book. Better, it is **a gentle straightforward guide that addresses dealmaker relationship concepts** that, if allowed, can only result with improving your life and your family."
      - Shirley Jobe on *Amazon.com*

"...short, manageable chapters with points of action at the end of each to help you put the subject matter into practice. **I would highly recommend it** to other wives."
      - Leslie Fisher on *Goodreads*

"[Jennifer's] book helps you to think about your motives, actions, thinking, and speaking. **I love it!**"
      - Shandra Pettway on *Amazon.com*

# 25 Ways to
# Communicate Respect
# to Your Husband

9.9.23
yanique

# 25 Ways to Communicate Respect to Your Husband

(a handbook for wives)

## *Jennifer Flanders*

Prescott Publishing

*25 Ways to Communicate Respect to Your Husband.*
Copyright ©2013 by Jennifer Flanders.

ISBN: 978-1-938945-02-1
LCCN: 2013920372

FIRST EDITION
10 9 8 7 6 5 4 3 2 1

*For Doug*
*whose wisdom and integrity*
*make him so easy to respect*

# - Contents -

# Introduction

Respect. Honor. Admiration. Esteem.

These are things all of us desire, but for men, the longing is particularly well ingrained. That is just the way they are wired.

Whether young or old, educated or uneducated, driven or laidback, single or married—a man craves respect. He wants to know that his friends, his family, and his coworkers trust his judgment, recognize his abilities, and value his opinions.

Nowhere is this truer than in marriage.

Your husband wants to know that you'll always be in his corner. That you're on his team. That you believe in him. And it's your job, as his wife, to assure him of those things.

Ephesians 5:33 tells us, *"the wife must see to it that she respects her husband."*

The Amplified Bible goes even further: *"Let the wife see that she respects and reverences her husband [that she notices him, regards him, honors him, prefers him, venerates, and esteems him; and that she defers to him, praises him, and loves and admires him exceedingly]."*

"Respect is one of the greatest expressions of love."

— Miguel Angel Ruiz

That's a tall order, isn't it?

Unfortunately, it's an area that needs a lot of work in a lot of marriages.

Some women think these scriptures are outdated and irrelevant; they seem bound and determined *not* to show respect to their husbands. "I'm just as important as he is," they argue, "*he* should be paying respect to *me*."

But even Christian wives—women who believe the Bible and sincerely try to live by it—often struggle with this concept.

Why is that?

I believe the problem for both groups of women stems from a lack of understanding. We don't understand the meaning of respect (its implications), and we don't know how or why to communicate respect (the applications).

# Introduction - Show Some Respect

Before we talk about what respecting your husband means, let's consider what it doesn't mean:

- Being respectful to your husband doesn't mean you're inferior to him.
- Being respectful to your husband doesn't mean you're not as smart as he is.
- Being respectful to your husband does not mean you are less capable than he is.
- Being respectful to your husband doesn't mean you are a doormat.
- Being respectful to your husband doesn't make you his slave.
- Being respectful to your husband doesn't mean you can't think for yourself.
- Being respectful to your husband doesn't mean you always agree with him.

So what does showing respect really entail?

My Oxford Dictionary contains two definitions for the word "respect."

The first is "to admire someone deeply, as a result of his abilities, qualities, or achievements." This is the sort of respect a wife should (ideally) feel for her husband—the sort her husband should (ideally) work hard to earn and maintain.

And in truth, many men do purposefully try to order their lives so as to ensure the continued admiration of their wives. If your husband is among them, you should thank him for making your job that much easier.

But even the best of husbands have flaws. If you wait for your husband to be perfect before showing him any respect, you will be waiting a long time.

Our husbands are all sinners (as are we). They all make mistakes (as do we). And it is entirely possible that their behavior may not always warrant our admiration.

But do any of those facts exempt us from treating them respectfully?

No, they do not.

You cannot make your own obedience to Scripture contingent on somebody else's performance. You are responsible for your own actions and reactions.

So how can one imperfect person show respect to another imperfect person?

The dictionary definitions give us a clue.

The second meaning of the verb "respect" is "to show due regard for the feelings, wishes, rights, or traditions of others."

> "Respect for ourselves guides our morals, respect for others guides our manners."
>
> - Laurence Sterne

In this sense, respect is a courtesy we should be extending not only to our husbands, but to everyone else we encounter, as well.

Yes, it is nice when this courtesy is reciprocated (as indeed it should be), but it is not essential. We can be polite and respectful toward others—showing consideration for their rights and feelings rather than trampling upon them—even when they are impolite or disrespectful toward us. This sort of respect really reveals more about the giver than it does the receiver.

But feeling respect and demonstrating respect are two separate things. Actions speak louder than words.

# Introduction - Show Some Respect

You can say you respect your husband, but he'll have a hard time believing you unless your behavior backs it up.

That behavior—the way you act towards the man you married—broadcasts to him (as well as the rest of the world) whether your professed respect is merely lip service or is genuine and abiding.

What does respectful living look like?

In the following chapters, we'll discuss ways a wife can communicate respect without ever uttering a word.[1] These aren't hard-and-fast rules. They're not inflexible duties. They are merely suggestions for women who do, in fact, respect their husbands and want to show it.

Since men occasionally interpret our words or tones or actions as being disrespectful even when no disrespect is felt or intended, this is sometimes more easily said than done—hence, my list of twenty-five pointers for showing respect in ways that most husbands will find meaningful, gleaned from over twenty-six joyous years of marriage. My husband does not demand any of this from me, but he gladly and gratefully receives it as my gift to him, just because it makes me happy to make him happy.

> "There is no respect for others without humility in one's self."
>
> - Henri Frederic Amiel

This is your invitation to sow these same seeds of happiness in your home by demonstrating respect for the man you married. If you'll make it a habit to do these things, then next time you tell your husband how much you respect him, he won't have to wonder if you really mean it.

## Put It into Practice:

- ✎ Copy Ephesians 5:33 (AMP) onto an index card and commit it to memory: "Let the wife see that she respects and reverences her husband [that she notices him, regards him, honors him, prefers him, venerates, and esteems him; and that she defers to him, praises him, and loves and admires him exceedingly]." Make it your goal to live by these words.

- ✎ Invite a couple of friends to read this book and discuss it with you. Hold one another accountable for applying what you learn.

- ✎ Consider focusing on each of these twenty-five areas for a week at a time. That way, you can give one a chance to become a habit before tackling the next. In the course of six months, you'll have worked your way through the whole list.

Chapter 1

It's true. A happy wife makes a happy life.

I suspect this quote was originally meant as a warning to hapless husbands: Do whatever it takes to keep your wife happy, because if she's not, she'll make your life miserable.

That, sadly, is how life falls out in a lot of marriages. Wives use moodiness as a way to manipulate and control their husbands, which is a crying shame (no pun intended).

But, fortunately for all concerned, this concept also works in reverse. Having a pleasant, joyful, happy wife will automatically make the rest of a man's life seem happier, fuller, and more satisfying.

Did you know that we wives have the power to do just that? To transform our homes from what might have been a vortex of negativity and darkness and despair into a refuge of joy and radiance and hope?

> "I am determined to be cheerful and happy in whatever situation I may find myself. For I have learned that the greatest part of our happiness depends on our dispositions, not our circumstance."
>
> - Martha Washington

Shouldn't we be using that power for good?

The answer is yes. Yes, we should.

One author goes so far as to suggest that, for the sake of our loved ones, we have a moral obligation to be as happy as possible.[1]

In other words, it's our duty to maintain a cheerful disposition.

That's because our outlook on life has a profound effect not only on our own happiness, but on the happiness of our husband and children, as well.

We do our family a grave disservice when we cultivate a perpetually sad or sour disposition. Such a disposition has little to do with life circumstances, and everything to do with choice, for as Abraham Lincoln once noted, "most people are about as happy as they make up their minds to be."

When I say that wives should "choose joy," I am not suggesting that we be dishonest, "fake," or insincere. Being joyful is not about smiling on the outside when we are shattered on the inside. It is not about pretending that life is hunky-dory when serious problems exist and we need help.

Choosing joy is not about putting on a show for another person's sake. It is about changing the way we look at things—for our own sake.

Being joyful is not about repressing feelings, but about attacking negativism at the root—in our heart and mind and attitudes. It is about being selective in our thoughts.

In every circumstance in life, there can be found something good, as well as something bad. Being joyful is about choosing to dwell on the good instead of on the bad.

> "There is only one way to happiness and that is to cease worrying about things which are beyond the power of our will."
>
> - Epictetus

It's about being glad for what we have instead of upset over what we don't.

That Scripture would repeatedly adjure us to rejoice implies that joy is indeed a choice:

- *"Rejoice in the Lord always; again I will say, rejoice!"* (Philippians 4:4)
- *"Always be joyful."* (1 Thessalonians 5:16, NLT)
- *"Consider it all joy, my brethren, when you encounter various trials, knowing that the testing of your faith produces endurance."* (James 1:2-3)
- *"Rejoice and be glad, for your reward in heaven is great..."* (Matthew 5:12)

This sort of constant, abiding joy has at its root an outward rather than an inward focus.

It asks not, "What can others do to make me happy," but "what can I do to make others happy?" Personal happiness is seldom the result of the former mindset, but it is a natural byproduct of the latter.

> "Whoever is happy will make others happy, too."
>
> - Mark Twain

Showing kindness to others and doing things to bring happiness to those around us is one of the surest ways to find happiness ourselves.

As Helen Keller so wisely observed, "Happiness cannot come from without. It must come from within. It is not what we see and touch or that which others do for us which makes us happy; it is that which we think and feel and do, first for the other fellow and then for ourselves."

You want to live happily ever after? It's never too late to begin. The choice is yours; choose joy.

4

## Put It into Practice:

- ✎ Margaret Bonnano once said, "It is only possible to live happily ever after on a day-to-day basis." What does that mean to you, and how should it affect how you live your life?

- ✎ Make a "Blessings Journal" by writing down all the things that bring you joy. Review this list and add to it often.

- ✎ Write the text of Philippians 4:4-8 and James 1:2-3 on flashcards to post on your refrigerator or in some other prominent location. You might even make extras to use as bookmarks. Commit these verses to memory and meditate on them frequently.

- ✎ If you do not already know them, learn the words to the hymn "Joyful, Joyful, We Adore Thee" or to the praise chorus, "Rejoice in the Lord Always, and Again I Say Rejoice." Sing them whenever you need a reminder.

- ✎ When life's trials and troubles try to steal your joy, look for ways that God might use those very things for your good and His glory. Stay focused on that silver lining rather than the looming storm.

# Chapter 2

A wife should give weight to what her husband thinks is important. She should make those things a priority that matter most to him, whether it's having dinner ready when he gets home from work or keeping the house tidy or limiting computer time.

When a wife blesses her husband by honoring his wishes, she finds herself being blessed in ways she never would have imagined.

Don't believe me?

The little book you are now reading is a good case in point. It was only by my choosing to honor the wishes of my husband that this book came into existence in the first place.

Here is how it happened:

I enjoy writing and had for a couple of years been trying my hand at blogging. However, my husband had grown increasingly concerned that the time I was devoting to my blog, *Loving Life at Home*, was causing me to neglect more important duties, so he asked me to limit my blogging to about 15 minutes a day.

> "Let honor be to us as strong an obligation as necessity is to others."
>
> - Pliny the Elder

Now 15 minutes a day may not sound like much, but as my husband explained, "If the Lord is in it, He can choose to bless your blog without your burning the candle at both ends. If not, then all your work is in vain, anyway, because nobody will ever read it." (And, in fact, very few people *were* reading it at the time.)

So I honored my husband's request. Not because I completely agreed with his assessment that I was just wasting my time, but because I earnestly desired (both then and now) to be obedient to Scripture and to really *live* by the ideals I promote on my blog and in my books.

Nevertheless, I continued to wrestle internally with what exactly it means for me to honor and respect my husband, and with how I can most effectively communicate with him that I do, in fact, hold him in the highest regard. At the same time, I began to compile a little list of reminders for myself.

The more I reviewed this little list, and the more I meditated on the Scriptures that back it up, the more convinced I became that this was something other wives might find helpful, as well.

So—after working in 15-minute-per-day increments for about three or four days—I published a new post on my blog: "25 Ways to Communicate Respect to Your Husband (Without Ever Uttering a Word)"

It was the very first post I'd written since my husband had told me God could bless my blog without my having to spend inordinate amounts of time on it.

"The greatest way to live with honor in this world is to be what we pretend to be."

\- Socrates

And do you know what? That is exactly what happened!

With that single post, *Loving Life at Home* went from getting 40-50 hits/day to getting 40-50 thousand hits/day. At this writing, that one article alone has been viewed well over a million times, pinned on Pinterest over 250K times, liked on Facebook 15K times, and tweeted, shared, and reblogged more times than I can count.

The point is, God blesses the wife who honors her husband. And one of the simplest ways a wife can do that is to honor her husband's wishes—not out of compulsion, as if she were his slave, but willingly and joyfully, as a means of demonstrating thoughtfulness and placing another person's happiness ahead of her own.

If this concept sounds foreign to you, it shouldn't. Mothers the world over take great pleasure in doing things that delight their children. Why shouldn't a wife give the same kind of consideration to her husband? Why shouldn't she seek to do the things she knows will please and delight and surprise the man she claims to love?

> "Love one another with brotherly affection. Outdo one another in showing honor."
>
> - Romans 12:10 ESV

It is this sort of selfless love the Bible is describing when it tells us, *"Do not merely look out for your own personal interests but also for the interests of others."* (Philippians 2:4)

That passage goes on to say that we should consider others as more important than ourselves. Such consideration will go a long way in communicating honor and respect toward your husband.

## Put It into Practice:

- ✍ It is impossible to honor someone's wishes if you don't know what those wishes are, so talk to your husband about his priorities for you and his goals for the family.

- ✍ Ask him to compile a short list (3-5 things) that he would most like to see you work on, then address those areas cheerfully and consistently.

- ✍ Make a habit of thinking, "What would my husband do?" or "What would he have me do?" when making decisions.

- ✍ "Ease and honor are seldom bedfellows"—or so the saying goes. Remember that next time you're faced with a choice of honoring your husband's wishes or doing the easier, more expedient thing. Take the high road, even if it's inconvenient to do so.

- ✍ Memorize Romans 12:10 in the ESV—"Love one another with brotherly affection. Outdo one another in showing honor."

- ✍ Brainstorm some ways you might "outdo" your husband in showing honor. Write them down. Picture yourself doing these things faithfully and cheerfully, then follow through until such behavior becomes second-nature.

# Chapter 3

As much as possible, try to give your husband your undivided attention. Lay other tasks aside, look into his eyes, and listen to what he is saying with the goal of understanding and remembering his words.

You honor your spouse when you attend to his voice: listening is a gift every wife should give her husband gladly.

But make sure you are listening *actively*, with your mind fully engaged in the conversation, as opposed to *passively*, where your ears hear the sounds that are coming out of your husband's mouth, but your brain doesn't really register his words.

I don't know about you, but passive listening is something I tend to do when I'm working at my computer. My children know this, which is why they pick that precise time to ask permission to do things I'd never allow if I were actually paying attention to their requests instead of distractedly nodding my head as I continue typing away at my keyboard.

> "Give whatever you are doing and whoever you are with the gift of your attention."
>
> - Jim Rohn

Then later, when I discover what they've been up to and demand an explanation, they offer an ironclad defense: "But we *did* ask, Mom, and you said it was okay!"

The lesson?

Fold down that laptop and focus on the person in front of you, because passive listening just won't cut it. Passive listening is hardly listening at all.

We need to be active and engaged listeners. We need to pay earnest attention. This is especially true when our husband is involved.

It's a skill that gets better with practice, provided we know what we're shooting for. The chart at the top of the next page will help you help differentiate between active and passive listening. Which kind of listener are you?

| *An Active Listener...* | *A Passive Listener...* |
|---|---|
| focuses on what's being said | daydreams until it's her turn to talk |
| lets words sink in and register | takes words in one ear, out the other |
| remains present and engaged | seems to be a million miles away |
| listens with an open heart/ mind | is fixated on her own opinions |
| tries to see other's point of view | remains stubbornly unconvinced |
| follows speaker's train of thought | mentally rehearses her own response |
| seeks a clearer understanding | seeks an end to the conversation |

Now, I realize that some couples enjoy idle chitchat as they work side by side on some chore or project. If they stopped working to look into each other's eyes whenever either uttered a word, progress would come to a complete standstill. I get that.

> "A little bit of attention can go a long way."
>
> - Nicholas Kristof

Sometimes it is neither practical nor feasible to drop everything in favor of making eye contact, but you can still communicate attentiveness by commenting on what is being said, asking questions, and stealing occasional glances at one another as you work.

Fortunately, women are masters of multi-tasking. It's possible to pay attention to one thing while doing another, a fact I demonstrated in school by crocheting during class.

Having something for my hands to do helped keep my mind from wandering and allowed me to concentrate on whatever lecture I was attending. My grades were good, and none of my instructors ever

*15*

questioned this practice until my second semester of graduate school, when my Numerical Analysis professor could not abide my doing needlework while he was teaching. So he wrote a note across the top of one of my test papers demanding that I "please stop knitting in class."

My grades suffered in consequence, until he finally relented and granted me special permission to crochet, provided I sat in the back of the classroom to do it. He came to realize that my staring at a blackboard was no guarantee I would actually see anything written upon it—especially not when my mind was a million miles away at the time.

> "There is no substitute for paying attention."
>
> - Diane Sawyer

Nor is looking a person straight in the eyes a guarantee that you will hear a single word he is saying—certainly not when your mind remains absorbed in your own thoughts or you use your partner's talking time as an opportunity to plot what you are going to say in response.

We don't get points for pretending to pay attention when we really aren't.

So focus on what your husband is saying. Allow his words to sink in and fully register. Listen... and let him know you are listening.

Lee Iacocca once said, "No matter what you've done for yourself or for humanity, if you can't look back on having given love and attention to your own family, what have you really accomplished?"

# Chapter 3 - Pay Attention

When you look back on the amount of love and attention you've given your spouse and children, are you satisfied that you've given your best?

Or are you plagued with regrets?

Commit afresh today to giving your loved ones the valuable, irreplaceable gift of your full attention and affection.

## Put It into Practice:

✍ Paul Tillich wrote, "The first duty of love is to listen." Tune your ears to listen for your husband's voice. Whenever you hear him speaking, perk up and pay attention! Train you children to do the same.

✍ Orchestrate your day so that tasks that require your undivided attention are completed while the rest of your family is asleep or away from home for school or work. That way, when you are together, you can be fully engaged—body, soul, and spirit.

✍ Don't make your husband compete with a smart phone or computer screen for your attention. When he is around, log off, power down, and be available.

✍ Next time your husband tries to tell you something, make a point to put down whatever you are working on and look him in the eyes to listen. Idle chitchat aside, some conversations warrant such a response.

## Chapter 4

Have you ever been around a person who won't let you finish a sentence? That gets really old really fast. Even if you think you already know what your husband is going to say, giving him the opportunity to say it without cutting him off mid-sentence shows both respect and common courtesy.

I am blessed to be married to a man who possesses an extraordinary gift for gab. My husband loves to talk. What's more, he is an animated storyteller, extremely articulate, and always has something interesting to say. I could listen to him all day and would be perfectly content to let him do most of the talking.

This is not the case in many marriages.

The vast majority of husbands are far less verbally expressive than their wives: the average woman uses 20,000 words per day, while the average man uses only 7000.[1] He comes home from work with his word bank depleted, while she's barely getting started.

> " There cannot be greater rudeness than to interrupt another in the current of his discourse."
>
> - John Locke

If this describes your husband, if he takes the time to really ponder what he is going to say before he says it, then it is especially important for you to practice patience and not interrupt as he tries to collect his thoughts and then put them into words.

Listening closely goes hand-in-hand with not cutting him off.

Have you ever been tempted to interrupt as a way to *prove* you are paying attention? To show that you know your husband so well, you can predict what he's going to say next? To communicate excitement and enthusiasm over the topic under discussion?

Resist that urge, because interrupting is rude and can be extremely annoying to the person interrupted.

Plus, the Bible warns repeatedly not to speak too much or answer too hastily:

- *"He who gives an answer before he hears—it is folly and shame to him."* (Proverbs 18:13)

## Chapter 4 - Don't Interrupt

- *"But everyone must be quick to hear and slow to speak..."* (James 1:19)
- *"Do you see a man who is hasty in his words? There is more hope for a fool than for him."* (Proverbs 29:20)
- *"Do not be quick with your mouth...let your words be few."* (Ecclesiastes 5:2)
- *"The one who has knowledge uses words with restraint...."* (Proverbs 17:27 NIV)
- *"He who guards his mouth and his tongue, guards his soul from troubles."* (Proverbs 21:23)
- *"When there are many words, transgression is unavoidable, but he who restrains his lips is wise."* (Proverbs 10:19)

That final verse touches on an important corollary to the notion that we should not interrupt: we also should not talk so much that we tempt *others* to interrupt.

No matter how quiet or introverted the person with whom you are attempting to visit, do not monopolize the conversation. Try to take an occasional break from talking. Pause

> "I haven't spoken to my wife in years. I didn't want to interrupt her."
>
> - Rodney Dangerfield

frequently enough to at least give him an opportunity to respond, even if it means just sitting in silence for a few moments.

This, again, is simply good manners. Plus, it helps to draw reluctant participants into the conversation.

My husband always used a similar trick to encourage our infants to vocalize. He'd lean over and make eye contact, then say something happy to our tiny baby and wait with an expectant smile on his face for the baby to "answer back." It sometimes took a few tries, but the babies quickly caught on and took great delight in so "conversing" with their daddy.

Children of all ages are more apt to communicate when we ask open-ended questions and wait with genuine interest to hear their response—and the same thing may be said of many husbands.

## Put It into Practice:

✍ Don't assume you always know what your husband is going to say before he says it. Maybe you do; maybe you don't. Instead of completing his sentences for him, wait and see if what he actually says is what you expected him to say. He might just surprise you.

✍ The dinner table is a great place to practice good listening skills. Be sure to involve your kids in the conversation, as well, and teach them to take turns talking: no interrupting and no monopolizing!

✍ If work schedules cause you to be separated from your husband for most of the day, then write yourself reminders about what you want to tell him when you are both together again: random thoughts to share, questions to ask, funny things that happen, etc. The list will later allow you to listen as he tells you about his day without fear of forgetting the things you want to tell him about yours. My husband often jots such notes to himself, then goes through the list point-by-point when he comes in from work. This habit makes me so happy. It tells me that he's thinking of me while he's away and looks forward to visiting with me when he gets home.

Emphasize His
Good Points

# Chapter 5

Sure, he has his faults (as do you), but dwelling on them will only make you both miserable. Choose instead to focus on the qualities in your husband that you most admire.

Scripture commands us: *"Whatever is true, whatever is honorable, whatever is right, whatever is pure, whatever is lovely, whatever is of good repute, if there is any excellence and if anything worthy of praise, dwell on these things."* (Philippians 4:8)

Certainly this verse applies to marriage as much as to any other facet of our life.

Again, it is a simple matter of treating others the way you want to be treated. Which would you prefer: That your husband focus his thoughts on your loveliest, most noble and praiseworthy characteristics? Or would you rather he ignore your good points completely and concentrate instead on your most annoying and bothersome flaws?

"If you fill your head with positive thoughts, there won't be any room left for negative ones."

-Orrin Woodward

Then do for him as you'd have him do for you.

Dwelling on the positive isn't so hard, especially when you consider that negative behaviors can sometimes stem from positive traits. Trace them back to their source.

Case in point: When we were first married, it often bothered me that my husband would make what I considered frivolous and impulsive purchases (back then, it was sodas and candy at the corner gas station, later it would be new cars and cutting-edge technologies).

But I eventually came to realize that my husband's spending habits go hand-in-hand with his giving habits: figuratively, since he views money as a tool, not as a treasure to be clutched or loved or horded; but also literally, because he usually gives away to some grateful person in need whatever good-as-new thing he is upgrading or replacing.

That lavish generosity, that willingness to share God's blessings with those around him, that ability to give cheerfully, hilariously even, is something very good indeed. It is one of the traits I admire and appreciate most about my husband. And now I am reminded of that fact every time he buys something I think he shouldn't.

It's okay for us to be different. His strengths are not my strengths, and vice versa. Much of this is by design, as God intends for man and woman to complement one another. Different is not necessarily bad. It is just... different.

So don't focus on the areas where you are strong, but your husband is weak—areas where, in your opinion, perhaps he doesn't quite measure up.

That focus will lead only to contempt, bitterness, and resentment, which will deal a deathblow to your love and intimacy, if not to your marriage itself. Think instead on the areas where you are weak but your husband is strong, areas where he complements and completes you.

> "The more you point out someone else's flaws, the more you emphasize your own."
>
> - Justice Cabral

Is your husband flawed? Certainly. He is a sinner. (In the words of Elizabeth Elliot, "There isn't anything else to marry!" [1]) But beyond praying for him, that fact cannot—must not—be your focus.

"Persons are judged to be great because of the positive qualities they possess, not because of the absence of faults." [2]

So look for the good in your spouse. Search for it as you would search for buried treasure. And keep *those* traits at the forefront of your mind.

If focusing on the positive has been a struggle for you in the past, pray that God will help you see your husband with new eyes.

Praise and admire your spouse verbally and often. Are you glad God brought him into your life? Tell him so! Would you feel you were missing out without him? Let him know it!

Emphasize his good points in your thoughts and in your speech, and you will see more of the same flourish in his character, his life, and his manner.

## Put It into Practice:

- ✍ Keep a running list of those things you most admire about your husband. Verbalize your appreciation for those qualities, both publicly and privately.

- ✍ Compose a poem or song for your husband that incorporates all the qualities from your above list. Save it for a special occasion, or surprise him with it for no reason at all.

- ✍ Next time you become annoyed with your husband for some little thing, mentally review and rehearse your original little rhyme.

- ✍ Send your husband a text or leave him a handwritten note for several days in a row, praising him individually for each of those good points you so admire.

- ✍ Think about what originally attracted you and your husband to one another. Are those qualities still present? If so, rejoice! If not, focus your efforts on being the girl he first fell in love with, then the man he once was will likely make a reappearance.

## Chapter 6

Ruth Graham advises wives to "tell your mate the positive, and tell God the negative." Take your concerns to God. Faithfully lift up your husband in prayer every day, and you will likely notice a transformation not only in him, but in yourself, as well.

Of course, we needn't wait until there is some problem or disagreement before beginning this practice. A wife can and should routinely intercede on her husband's behalf. Prayer should be a habit of life, something we do continuously and "without ceasing." (1 Thessalonians 5:17)

We all need God's help, but husbands especially so, since as the head of their household, they have the concerns of the entire family resting on their shoulders.

Your husband is accountable before God not only for himself, but also for the way he leads and directs and serves and cares for his wife and children. That's a lot of responsibility.

Yet Scripture tells us, *"Be anxious for nothing, but in everything by prayer and supplication with thanksgiving let your requests be made known to God. And the peace of God, which surpasses all comprehension, will guard your hearts and your minds in Christ Jesus."* (Philippians 4:6-7)

"Any concern too small to be turned into a prayer is too small to be made into a burden."

- Corrie Ten Boom

Now that is a promise too good to ignore!

There are many different daily, weekly, or monthly plans available that can help make praying for your husband more systematic.

You can pray for him in all his different roles: spouse, father, son, brother, teacher, coach, counselor, and employee.

You can pray for his character development, focusing on one attribute a day as you pray through various lists given in Scripture, such as the fruit of the Spirit (Galatians 5:22-23), the beatitudes from the Sermon on the Mount (Matthew 5:1-12), or the defining attributes of love (1 Corinthians 13).

*32*

Or you can use a plan I heard about several years ago and pray for your husband from head to toe:

- **Pray for his brain**—that God would keep it sharp and focused and that his thoughts would not be conformed to this world, but would be transformed and renewed by the power of God. (Romans 12:2)
- **Pray for his eyes**—that he would guard them diligently and would set no worthless thing before them. (Psalm 101:3)
- **Pray for his ears**—that they'd be tuned to hear God's still, small voice and would remain attentive to the Holy Spirit's promptings. (1 Thessalonians 5:19; Isaiah 30:9)
- **Pray for his mouth**—that no unwholesome talk would proceed from it, but only what is good for building others up. Pray that he would always and only speak the truth in love. (Ephesians 4:15, 29)
- **Pray for his arms**—that God would strengthen them and make them firm. Pray that he'd take delight in his labor and that God would bless the work of his hands. (Psalm 90:17, Ecclesiastes 3:22)
- **Pray for his heart**—that Christ would sit enthroned upon it, that your husband would love God with all his heart and soul and might, that he'd love his neighbor as himself. (Mark 12:30-31) Pray for his heart to remain soft toward you (Proverbs 5:18-19) and to be knitted to the hearts of his children. (Malachi 4:6)

- **Pray for his legs**—that God would strengthen and give him stamina, so he can run with endurance the race that is set before him, without growing weary or fainting along the way. (Hebrews 12:1; Isaiah 40:31)
- **Pray for his feet**—that they'd be quick to flee from temptation, to turn away from evil, and to faithfully pursue righteousness, wisdom, peace, love, and truth. (2 Timothy 2:22; Psalm 34:14; Proverbs 4:5-7)

Praying for your husband not only enlists the enabling power of God, but it encourages you to give thought to how you might improve the situation yourself.

If, for instance, you are asking God to ease his financial burdens, you could brainstorm ways you might spend less, contribute more, or to drum up new business for him. While praying that God would help your husband control his temper, you should also purpose to quit intentionally doing things that you know will aggravate him.

In other words, we should "get on our knees and pray, then get on our feet and work."[1]

## Put It into Practice:

- ✎ Pray for your husband in all his different roles: husband, father, son, believer, provider, neighbor, brother, etc.

- ✎ Visit my website (*http://lovinglifeathome.com*) and print a copy of "Praying for Your Husband from Head to Toe." Use it as a reminder every day this week to cover your spouse in prayer.

- ✎ Pray for your husband's reputation. Pray that he would value a good name more than riches. (Proverbs 22:1) Ask God to make him a man of integrity.

- ✎ Next time you are angry or irritated with your spouse, try praying for him instead of arguing.

- ✎ If he is agreeable, set aside time every day to pray with your husband—over coffee before work each morning, before turning into bed every night, or whatever other time fits your schedules.

- ✎ Pray for your husband's business ventures. Pray that he would meet success with humility, and pray that he would face failure with determination, in faith that God can use even financial setbacks for good.

Don't Nag

Chapter 7

Your husband is a grown man, so don't treat him like a two-year-old. Leave room for God to work. You are not the Holy Spirit, so do not try to do His job.

Although husbands can be forgetful and a gentle reminder may sometimes be welcomed—or even specifically requested—constant unsolicited pestering about something you've already discussed at length is rarely appreciated.

Does it bother you that your spouse does not always respond to matters with the same sense of urgency you feel? Perhaps he is stalling so that he can think through the situation more clearly. Or maybe he disagrees with you on the course of action a circumstance warrants.

Either way, it would be prudent to give the man a little space.

When my husband and I were first married, I would sometimes get in a mood where I wanted to tell him exactly how something he was doing should (or shouldn't) be done. Not in a calm, collected, you-might-consider-trying-it-this-way fashion, but in a high-strung, insistent, my-way-is-the-only-right-way tone of voice.

That never went over very well, although I must admit, my husband had a brilliant way of dealing with me during such times. He'd simply say, "You're so sweet," give me a kiss, and change the subject. We were married ten years before I realized "You're so sweet" was his secret code for "You're such a nag."[1]

> "People have a way of becoming what you encourage them to be, not what you nag them to be."
> - Author Unknown

Unfortunately, many husbands do not respond to nagging with the same patience and grace that mine demonstrated. Then again, many husbands have had to deal with a higher volume of nagging to start with. That would wear on any man's nerves.

The Bible tells us about a wife named Delilah, who *"tormented [her husband] with her nagging day after day until he was sick to death of it."* (Judges 16:16

*NLT*) Another translation says she "pestered him until he wished he were dead."[2] Elsewhere, the verb is translated "vexed," "annoyed," "wearied," or "tired to death."

Her husband, Samson, finally gave in to all her nagging. The story did not end well for anybody involved, but that is not my point.

My point is that this wife was treating her husband in a manner that vexed, annoyed, and wearied him until he was sick of her, sick of marriage, and sick of life itself.

Why would any woman choose to behave that way?

Contentious wives do far more complaining than praying. Can the same be said of you? If so, try giving up the persistent nagging in favor of persistent prayer, and see if that isn't much more effective in the long run.

> "We're building up or tearing down in everything we do. Are you a part of the construction gang or on the wrecking crew?"
>
> - Author Unknown

Ultimately, only God can change hearts. If there is something that you are concerned about, or if you disagree, prayer would be a better use of your time and energies.

A patient, gentle, and loving attitude goes much farther than a critical, faultfinding, or demanding demeanor, as noted in the following comment from one of my readers:

*"I've learned that being flexible, adaptable and giving has increased my husband's love for me and he is happy to give in to things that I want. There is no need for nagging, competition, and other things that tear apart marriages."*

This is not the dynamic we see portrayed in media these days. In almost every sitcom made in the past thirty years, men are portrayed as being inept idiots who would be completely lost if not for the smart, sassy, savvy women in their lives. Husband/wife relationships are portrayed as being especially dysfunctional.

Aren't you thankful you don't have to accept Hollywood's version of reality? Aren't you glad you don't have to settle for the status quo?

God has provided a much better way for husbands and wives to relate to one another. Leave off the nagging, stop treating your husband like a child, and speak to him in a dignified and respectful manner. Season your words with grace and cover your conversations in prayer.

## Put It into Practice:

✎ I heard the story of one husband who quietly purposed to give his wife $20 if she could go one full day without nagging him. Since she knew nothing of his intent, it took over six months for her to earn the reward. Try pretending there's $20 riding on your ability to resist the urge to nag, and see how long it would take you to earn it.

✎ Take a look at the "Honey-Do List" that tempts you to nag your husband about household chores. Why not tend to as many of the items as you can yourself? Not in a showy, look-at-me-I'm-such-a-martyr sort of way, but in a helpful, quiet, I-want-to-take-as-much-off-your-plate-as-I-can manner.

✎ Let go of your notions of fairness. Marriage is not a 50/50 proposition, as so many allege. Give 110%, and refuse to harbor resentment if you perceive your husband is giving less.

✎ When nagging has been a way of life, it can be easy to slide back into it, even when you don't intend to. Enlist your husband's help in your efforts to change. Give him permission to tell you if he senses you're slipping back into old habits. "You're so sweet" works for us (now that I know what it really means), but you can use any phrase that will serve as a gentle reminder of your commitment to stop.

Be
Thankful

# Chapter 8

We need to cultivate an attitude of gratitude. Giving thanks is something that we are commanded repeatedly in Scripture to do. Obviously, it is important to God for His children to be grateful.

Space won't permit me to list all the references here, but consider this small sampling of verses:

- *"In everything give thanks; for this is God's will for you in Christ Jesus."* (1 Thessalonians 5:18)

- *"Whatever you do in word or deed, do all in the name of the Lord Jesus, giving thanks through Him to God the Father."* (Colossians 3:17)
- *"Always giving thanks for all things in the name of our Lord Jesus Christ ..."* (Ephesians 5:20)
- *"Oh give thanks to the LORD, call upon His name...."* (1 Chronicles 16:8)
- *"Enter His gates with thanksgiving.... Give thanks to Him, bless His name."* (Psalm 100:4)

We owe a debt of gratitude to God, but this attitude should also spill over into our relationships with others, as well. Our lives and our conversations should be marked by expressions of thankfulness toward our fellow man.

> "As we express our gratitude, we must never forget that the highest appreciation is not to utter words, but to live by them."
>
> - John F. Kennedy

And that goes double for the members of our own household.

Don't take your husband for granted. Express genuine appreciation for everything he does for you, whether great or small. Always say thank you.

But don't stop there. Real gratitude runs much deeper than words. It extends far beyond anything we can verbalize. Our thankfulness should affect not only how we think, but also how we live and how we treat the people around us.

Be forewarned: there are two things that will snuff out gratitude faster than blowing out a candle, and we must guard our hearts against both.

Those two things are envy and expectations.

Envy causes us to see the glass as half-empty instead of half-full. It fills our hearts with jealousy and bitter resentment, so that we begrudge others the good things they enjoy and pity ourselves for not sharing the same fate.

> "The mortal enemies of gratitude and contentment are envy and expectations."
>
> - Jennifer Flanders

Nothing will blind you faster to your own blessings more effectively than moping over what you lack, rather than rejoicing over what you have. If you can't even recognize or acknowledge all the good things in your life, then you certainly won't feel proper appreciation for them.

Expectations can deal as serious a deathblow to gratitude as envy does, for expectations give rise to a sense of entitlement.

It is impossible to feel truly grateful for something when you're convinced you deserve it. You can't sincerely appreciate anything if you think someone owes it to you.

Expectations have destroyed a lot of marriages, and it's not difficult to understand why.

Imagine for a moment that it's your anniversary. Your husband brings you flowers...but you were hoping for diamonds. You've been hinting for weeks and had even left a marked catalog on his desk. Doesn't he know this is the year for diamonds?

He probably bought these flowers at the grocery store on his way home from work. What a slacker! Can't he ever plan ahead? Why are special occasions always an afterthought with him?

Before long, you are really miffed. Your husband can see this in your eyes, sense it in your tone of voice—and it stings. He does something nice for you, and this is how you react? Whatever happened to a simple thank you? Why does he even bother trying?

> "Feeling gratitude and not expressing it is like wrapping a present and not giving it."
>
> - William Arthur Ward

He stews until he's boiling, then spends your wedding anniversary sleeping on the couch.

Life doesn't have to be like this.

Let's try that scenario again, but this time when your husband brings home flowers, you are delighted. He's been so busy at work lately, you're surprised he remembered your anniversary at all. What a sweetheart!

You hug his neck, give him a long kiss, and thank him profusely. You arrange the bouquet in water, set it on the table, and stop to admire it every time you pass. Your husband sees you do this and smiles with pleasure.

You make sincere and repeated comments about how beautiful the flowers look, how wonderful they smell, and how blessed you are to be married to such a sweet and thoughtful guy—not just tonight, but for as long as the flowers last.

My question is, which wife will you choose to be? Which would your husband rather come home to?

## Put It into Practice:

✍ Continue adding to the "Blessing Journal" you began in Chapter 1. Big or small, write down the good things in your life, and then actively look for ways to acknowledge and express appreciation for them.

✍ Stock up on a nice supply of thank you notes and use them regularly. Take time to send written thanks, especially for gifts and hospitality. Let thankfulness become second nature. Make it a habit. Gratitude is more likely to spill over on your husband and children if it is how you relate to everyone you encounter.

✍ If you don't already know the hymns, "Count Your Blessings," or "Make Me a Channel of Blessing," learn the words and sing them often as a reminder to maintain that attitude of gratitude.

✍ Read through Psalms and count how many times we are commanded to give thanks, just in that book alone. (See especially Psalm 107, Psalm 118, and Psalm 136.)

✍ Do all you can to cultivate thankful hearts in your children, as well. Teach them to express gratitude, especially to their father. And model that behavior for them.

# Chapter 9

Bob Marley said, "The most beautiful curve on a woman's body is her smile."

I tend to agree.

A smile is a beautiful thing, in and of itself. Any face looks better when it is graced with a happy, heartfelt smile. A radiant smile can transform an otherwise plain visage into something extremely attractive (just as an angry scowl can turn an extremely attractive face into something downright repulsive).

A smile provides an instant facelift, at a fraction of the cost of the surgical variety—and it's faster, easier, safer, and far more natural looking, as well.[1]

What's more, smiles spread happiness. Studies have shown that smiles can even *create* happiness: "The nerves connected to your face's smile muscles project right into parts of the brain that help determine mood. Send a signal to your brain that you're happy, and *voila!* You are happy."[2]

There have been several interesting studies, in fact, which have examined the interplay between expressions and emotions. Many people assume that an emotion is felt first, and is then communicated by an expression on the face. But research indicates this process can also work in reverse: the emotion we feel can actually *be triggered* by the expression on our face.

"Sometimes your joy is the source of your smile, but sometimes your smile can be the source of your joy."

– Thích Nhất Hạnh

"The face is not a secondary billboard for our internal feelings," observes Malcolm Gladwell in *Blink*. "It is an equal partner in the emotional process."[3]

Bottom line? Smile frequently—even if you don't feel particularly happy—and the feelings will eventually follow.

A smile has the power not only to make you happy, but to make others happy, as well. That's because smiles are contagious. "Smile and the world smiles with you," as the saying goes.[4]

I've always been an avid people-watcher. It's an activity I enjoy whenever I'm at the park or the pool or any other public place. Not in a stalking, staring, break-out-the-binoculars mode or manner, but in an attentive, alert, always aware-of-my-surroundings sort of way.

I especially enjoy observing the interactions between husbands and wives or between mothers and children. I've learned a lot by doing this over the years—gleaning wisdom from both positive and negative examples.

One thing I've discovered is that you needn't be close enough to eavesdrop to understand what's being said. Body language broadcasts it all, loud and clear.

> "If you smile when no one else is around, you really mean it."
>
> – Andy Rooney

That's a good thing to remember when you're out and about with your own family. You never know when somebody might be watching, learning, taking notes, or—in the present age of smart phones—video taping!

That's one reason I try not to do anything in public I wouldn't want broadcast on YouTube! But if I am behaving in such a way that I'd be embarrassed for complete strangers to watch my actions on the Internet, how much more should I want to spare my beloved family such scenes, both in public and at home?

It's important that we remember communication starts before a single word is uttered, before a solitary sound is intoned. It begins with attitude and posture, with body language and facial expressions. In fact, the actual words we speak constitute only seven percent of total communication. Facial expressions account for a full 55 percent and vocal tone makes up the additional 38 percent.[5]

Think about that fact, then ask yourself the question: What are my nonverbal cues saying to my husband? Is this really the message I *want* to send?

- furrowed brows
- distracted gaze
- rolled eyes
- grimace
- pursed lips
- angry scowl
- bored yawn
- indifferent stare
- raised brows
- dropped jaw
- narrow squint
- upturned nose
- heavy sigh
- clenched teeth
- perpetual frown
- deadpan glance
- crossed arms
- hardened jaw

In how many instances might a smile be just as easy, but a hundred times better? Next time, why not try smiling instead?

## Put It into Practice:

✍ Smile at your husband every day. Let your smile be the first thing he sees each morning and the last thing he sees before going to bed.

✍ Get in the habit of smiling every time you answer the telephone—even if you know it's just a telemarketer calling. The person on the other end of the line will hear the smile in your voice and be brightened by it.

✍ Take a lesson from Jacqueline Smith (one of the original *Charlie's Angels*), and find your best smile. I've never seen an unflattering photograph of this actress, nor a portrait in which she is not slightly facing left. Her smile is well practiced, yet warm, and she looks just as lovely in her late sixties as she did in her early twenties. When I first noticed that predictable tilt of her head, my own smile was far from polished—rather, it was stiff or strained or just plain goofy-looking. I quit even bringing school portraits home, to keep my parents from buying any immortalized reminders of my prolonged awkward stage. But with Jacqueline's example to guide me, I practiced in the mirror until I could consistently smile in a way that seems genuine and relaxed—and for the past couple of decades, that's the smile I've used anytime anyone's come at me with a camera. But a smile looks fake if it doesn't go all the way up to your eyes, so combat the pasted-on look by thinking happy thoughts when you practice smiling.

Respond
Physically

## Chapter 10

Here's a little pop quiz question for you. Say your husband sneaks up and squeezes you from behind. Do you:

    A. Tense up?
    B. Tell him off?
    C. Try to get away?
    D. Turn around and squeeze back!

Did you know that the way you respond (or don't respond) to your spouse's romantic overtures has a profound effect on his self-confidence?

Don't slap him away when he tries to hug you or make excuses when he's in the mood. Your enthusiastic cooperation and reciprocation will not only assure him of your love, but will make him feel well respected, too.

There are acceptable alternatives for taking care of every other need your husband has. Theoretically, somebody else could prepare his meals or clean his house or wash his laundry or care for his children, but you—*you!*—are the only person on earth who can rightfully address and fulfill his need for sexual intimacy.

Moreover, as his wife, you have a moral obligation to do so (just as your husband has a moral obligation to meet your sexual needs).

Women may not like being reminded of this fact, but the Bible spells it out very clearly:

> *"The husband must fulfill his duty to his wife, and likewise also the wife to her husband. The wife does not have authority over her own body, but the husband does; and likewise also the husband does not have authority over his own body, but the wife does. Stop depriving one another, except by agreement for a time, so that you may devote yourselves to prayer, and come together again so that Satan will not tempt you because of your lack of self-control."*
> (1 Corinthians 7:3-5)

There are many compelling reasons to prioritize sex with your husband, not only for his sake, but for your own sake, as well. In fact, I have devoted eleven full chapters (154 pages) of my book *Love Your Husband/ Love Yourself* to discussing all the physical, psychological, and emotional benefits of maintaining an active sex life in the context of marriage. It's a why-to book (not a how-to book), and wives who've read it are telling me it has completely changed their perspective. For the first time ever, rather than viewing marital sex as a duty, they've been able to see it for what it is and should be: a privilege and a delight.

A wife reaps as many benefits from an active sex life as her husband does. Time and space will not permit me to delve very deeply into all the supporting research here, but I will summarize it in the following broad categories:

- **Sex strengthens the marital bond:**
  Hormones released during sex help knit spouses' hearts and minds together.[1]
- **Sex improves health and boosts immunity:**
  Sex protects against heart disease, cancer, and a host of other illnesses.[2]
- **Sex calms and quiets the nerves:**
  Sex relieves anxiety very effectively and also acts as an anti-depressant.[3]
- **Sex allows for better rest:**
  An active sex life helps to promote deeper and more satisfying sleep.[4]
- **Sex makes for a happier home:**
  An active sex life reduces stress and rids our homes of tension and strife.[5]
- **Sex is a virtual fountain of youth:**
  An active sex life can boost your energy and make you look ten years younger.[6]
- **Sex provides an engaging pastime:**
  Sex as God designed it is great fun and should be enjoyed regularly.[7]

- **Sex is essential for growing a family:**
  Some of the best benefits of an active sex life are the babies that result from it.[8]
- **Sex helps guard against outside temptations:**
  An active sex life protects the long-term stability of your marriage.[9]
- **Sex lends credence to our testimony:**
  An active sex life assures our kids that it really *is* worth the wait to save sex for marriage.[10]

Some women (mistakenly) believe that if a wife has sex with her husband when she's not "in the mood," it is somehow a lie. I cannot count the number of responses I've received from readers who were of this opinion.

> "Waiting for the mood to strike is fine, as long as you make certain it strikes with predictable regularity. Otherwise, you should just go ahead and get started without it."
>
> – Jennifer Flanders

There are two problems with this line of thinking.

First of all, it's inconsistently applied. We do not think it is dishonest for a husband to hold down a job when he'd rather play hooky. On the contrary, we would consider it irresponsible if he *didn't* work hard to provide for his family. Likewise, if a mother gets up in the night to nurse her baby when she'd rather be sleeping, we don't accuse her of being a fraud. In fact, we'd consider it negligent if she *didn't* tend to her child's nutritional needs.

When you love someone, whether it is a spouse or a child or a friend, it is often necessary to put their needs ahead of your own—and love allows you to do it gladly. This is not being dishonest; it is showing consideration and compassion.

The second problem I see with requiring a wife to be "in the mood" before agreeing to sex is that, for women, willingness must often precede desire. That is just the way our brains are wired. One of my readers explains this dilemma very succinctly:

> *Regarding the sex thing, nine times out of ten, I don't feel like it. Once we start, it's usually lovely—there's a reason we married!—and afterwards I'm relaxed, happy, full of endorphins, and feel connected to my husband. If we waited for my libido fairy, who's generally cowed by fatigue and worry, we'd have sex twice a year.*[11]

This woman gets it. She admits that if she waited for the mood to hit *before* agreeing to sex, she'd only make love biannually—and she intuitively knows *that* extreme would not be good for her marriage.

I recognized this same dynamic fairly early in my own marriage. Having conceived just two short weeks into our honeymoon, my energy and libido suddenly dropped through the floor, and all I could think about was *sleep*.

Meanwhile, the only thing my husband seemed to think about was *sex*. We both spent our days counting the hours until we could crawl back in bed, but our ideas of what should happen once we got there differed dramatically!

I wish I could tell you that I considered his needs ahead of my own from the very beginning of our marriage, but that is sadly not the case. The truth is, I behaved very selfishly—every bit as selfishly, in fact, as I accused him of acting at the time.

It's a shortsighted wife who marginalizes or ignores her husband's need for physical intimacy. She cannot habitually deny him sex without it taking a toll on the happiness and stability of their marriage.

> "What counts in making a happy marriage is not so much how compatible you are, but how you deal with incompatibility."
>
> - Leo Tolstoy

True, a husband who has vowed to stick with his wife for better or worse is obligated before God to faithfully honor that promise, whether his wife is enthusiastically accommodating or sexually frigid, whether she treats him with heartfelt respect or utter disdain, whether she is a joy or a terror to live with. [12]

My question is, if I truly love my husband, why would I want to behave in a way that makes keeping his vows more a drudgery than a delight? Why test his resolve unnecessarily?

Why not, instead, make the most of every opportunity to reaffirm and reassure him of my own love and devotion—in a way that really speaks to him?

## Put It into Practice:

- ✍ If you're a parent and don't have a pickproof lock on your bedroom door, you need to get one ASAP. Go by your local hardware store and invest in a brass flip-lock. This simple device looks like a hinge, mounts easily and unobtrusively to the doorframe, works great, and only costs a couple of bucks—a small price to pay for privacy and peace of mind.

- ✍ Does your husband have a stronger sex drive than you do? Make it your goal to never turn him down again. (You don't have to tell him that's your plan, if you're afraid he'll be tempted to ask for sex three times a day… but then again, a little accountability might be good for both of you).

- ✍ Are you the spouse with the stronger drive? Don't be afraid to make the first move. If he needs more convincing, point him to the list of benefits on pages 57-58 and let him know he'll miss out on most of them if he doesn't cooperate.

Eyes Only
for Him

## Chapter 11

Getting married changes a lot more than the marital status of the bride and groom—it also affects every other relationship either spouse is involved in. Family dynamics shift, responsibilities change, and old friends take a backseat to the new spouse.

That's because marriage calls for a leaving and cleaving. When a man and woman become husband and wife, they should leave home and family behind—not just physically, but mentally and emotionally—as they begin to pour themselves into establishing a new family, building their own home, and investing in their joint future.

Roles change after marriage. Sure, family's still family, and we still love them, but the dynamic is different. No longer are we children under parental authority, bound by their rules and dependent upon their provision. Rather, we're mature adults who must make our own way and answer directly to God for the path we choose.

> "It is not someone else's responsibility to honor my marriage. It's my responsibility."
>
> – David Duchovny

But marriage doesn't only change the way we relate to our family, it also alters how we handle friendships. Not that our friends aren't still our friends, but time spent with them can no longer predominate our lives or free time.

This is especially true when it comes to male-female friendships.

Time spent together with friends of the opposite sex should probably be scaled back to zero, unless spouses are present. Such a practice would be consistent with traditional marriage vows, which include a pledge to "forsake all others and cling only unto thee."

If you want to safeguard your marriage and assure your husband of your undying love and devotion, then you must be extremely careful in the way you relate to, speak of, and think about other men.

# Chapter 11 - Eyes Only for Him

Once you're married, there is no room for flirting with anyone except your husband; you must be more guarded when interacting with the opposite sex. Let there be no ambiguity about your commitment to marriage in general or to your husband in particular.

Never compare your husband unfavorably to another man. It is neither fair nor respectful and will only breed trouble and discontent. Don't compare him to your:

| | |
|---|---|
| -father | -fellow workers |
| -father-in-law | -facebook followers |
| -family members | -fictional characters |
| -friends | -fantasy of ideal manhood |

Assure your husband that he has your whole heart. Affirm and admire him every chance you get. You may want to avoid even *positive* comparisons, because they still send the message that he is being measured against other men. This can cause feelings of insecurity, for if you make a habit of comparing your husband to others, he may fear that a comparison will eventually be made in which he'll be found lacking.

> "Jealousy is the fear of comparison."
>
> – Max Frisch

Take care not to rave too enthusiastically about a member of the opposite sex, real or imaginary. Many wives would feel slighted to hear their husband go on and on about how drop-dead gorgeous another woman is. Even if it were true, and the woman in question were strikingly beautiful, it would seem inappropriate for a married man to provide gushing commentary on that fact.

Likewise, most husbands would prefer not to hear the rapturous praise of another man being sung by their wife. If your eyes are going to light up when you speak about a man, you'd better be talking about the one you're married to.[1]

A wife should avoid watching movies or reading books that might cause her to stumble in this area, as well. Jesus said that when we lust in our heart after someone to whom we are not married, we are guilty of committing adultery. (Matthew 5:27-28) Notice that this warning applies as readily to women as it does to men.

> "Comparison is the death of joy."
>
> – Mark Twain

So before you pick up that romance novel, or buy that movie ticket, or pin that portrait of some shirtless star onto your (real or virtual) bulletin board, ask yourself whether doing so will be a snare and a trap to you. If so, choose the high road.

Pray with the psalmist, *"Let the words of my mouth and the meditation of my heart be acceptable in your sight, O LORD, my rock and my Redeemer."* (Psalm 19:14) The word for "meditation" may also be translated "thoughts." And there are many more verses that address the importance of our thought patterns:

- *"Guard your heart above all else, for it determines the course of your life."* (Prov. 4:23)
- *"For out of the heart come evil thoughts... adultery, sexual immorality.... These are what defile a person."* (Matthew 15:19-20)

## Chapter 11 - Eyes Only for Him

Having eyes only for your husband doesn't really start with your eyes. It begins with your heart and with your mind.

So take the battle there and prevail.

# Put It into Practice:

✍ It's good for married couples to develop friend-ships with other married couples. Look for couples who share and support your values and vision for family. Couples who are in the same season of life will be able to identify closely with your struggles, which can be good for encouragement and brainstorming, but you should also form friendships with older couples if possible—couples who are a little further down life's road and can point out the pitfalls and provide wise and godly counsel.

✍ When praising your husband, use comparisons only in the most general (and superlative) terms: "You're the sexiest man alive" is acceptable. "You're better looking than our mechanic" probably isn't. Let your husband's good qualities stand on their own merit rather than measuring him against a specific person. Build him up without tearing others down.

✍ If you've developed a habit of comparing your husband negatively to others, either verbally or mentally, turn over a new leaf. If faults must be addressed, do so prayerfully and respectfully without dragging anybody else into the picture.

✍ Are you on Pinterest? Be careful what you pin and who you follow. Does a married woman really need to collect photos of shirtless men, chiseled abs, and muscle-bound chests? Why?

Kiss Him
Goodbye

# Chapter 12

When I was in high school, an American musical duo by the name of Hall & Oates recorded a song that was immensely popular at the time. For over thirty years now, I've thought they were singing, "Your Kiss is on My Lips."

It wasn't until I began writing this chapter and bothered to look up the lyrics that I learned the title of the song is actually "Kiss on My List"—as in "*your kiss is on my list... of the best things in life.*" And you know what? I like those words even better!

The lyrics go on to say: *"Because your kiss (your kiss) I can't resist/ Because your kiss is what I miss when I turn out the light."*[1]

Shouldn't that be my goal as a wife? To make a habit of kissing my husband so often and so passionately that he would consider my kiss one of the best things in life? To routinely give him the kind of soft, sweet, sensual kisses that he finds irresistible? To make our nights together at home so memorable that he really misses me whenever we're apart?

> "A kiss is a lovely trick designed by nature to stop speech when words become superfluous."
>
> – Ingrid Bergman

I once read about an interesting study conducted in Germany. Researchers found that men whose wives kissed them goodbye every morning were more successful than men who weren't kissed.[2] A simple farewell kiss was the one consistent factor that set high achievers apart from the rest.

Can you imagine that?

The fact is, success and respect often go hand-in-hand, so if you want to communicate respect for your husband, be sure to send him off right, and don't forget to greet him with a kiss when he returns home, for good measure.

In addition to improving your husband's earning potential, kissing offers many powerful health incentives[3] —and these hold true for both participants:

- **Kissing prevents cavities and tooth decay** by increasing saliva production, which in turn helps to wash away plaque.
- **Kissing reduces stress and anxiety** by helping to lower blood pressure and relieve tension.
- **Kissing strengthens health and immunity** by triggering the release of oxytocin and many other disease fighting chemicals into the bloodstream.
- **Kissing counteracts the signs of aging** by firming up facial muscles, plumping lips, and precipitating a rosier, healthier complexion.
- **Kissing improves cardiovascular health** by raising your heart rate (at least potentially) and providing total body conditioning.
- **Kissing boosts confidence and self-esteem** by improving your state of mind, balancing your mood, and raising your happiness level.

And if all that is not reason enough to smooch your spouse, there is also this: Kissing fulfills a Biblical injunction. In 2 Corinthians 13:12, we are told very plainly to *"Greet one another with a holy kiss."*

With so many benefits riding on it, you'll want to pucker up at every opportunity!

"The sound of a kiss is not so loud as that of a cannon, but its echo lasts a great deal longer."

- Oliver Wendell Holmes

71

## Put It into Practice:

✎ Get up early enough to brush your teeth and swish a little mouthwash before your husband leaves for work, so you'll be ready to offer him a proper good-bye kiss at the door.

✎ Perhaps you are the one who's leaving home and returning later. It's still a great practice to seek him out before you go, tell him you're leaving and plant one on him.

✎ As one of my readers suggests, don't just limit your kissing to goodbyes. "Couples should also kiss each other hello. And goodnight. And OFTEN! Kissing is fun!"

Feed Him
His Favorites

## Chapter 13

Some people say that the quickest way to a man's heart is through his stomach. While that statement may not be anatomically or physiologically accurate, your husband obviously does need to eat and, given the choice, would probably prefer to dine on something he enjoys.

Taking your man's likes and dislikes into account when planning and preparing meals is a thoughtful way to demonstrate love for him and respect for his personal tastes.

Of course, this can be a little challenging when your spouse's tastes differ vastly from your own. Such is the case in my own marriage. My husband favors red meat that's been deep-fried, smothered in gravy, and/or wrapped in bacon. I prefer fresh fruit, raw veggies, and anything made with chocolate. My first pick off the menu would invariably be his last, and vice versa.

After sharing meals for more than a quarter of a century, though, I'm happy to report that we've both moved a little closer to center. I've learned to eat meat, and he will now tolerate beans, broccoli, and bell peppers.

> "When a man's stomach is full it makes no difference whether he is rich or poor."
>
> - Euripides

Even so, I usually save the soups and casseroles to eat with the kids for lunch when Dad's not home, then fix things at dinner he's sure to enjoy.

Although the rest of the family is not overly-fond of spaghetti, I know it's my husband's favorite, so I usually make it three or four times a month as a way to please and honor him. He also loves crispy tacos and cheese enchiladas, so both those dishes are regular staples at our house, as well.

It's possible that you don't do all or even most of the cooking for your family. Some couples eat out a lot or take turns making dinner, especially when both spouses work outside the home. Or maybe you married a man who loves to cook. I think if a man wants to spend hours in the kitchen creating culinary masterpieces, his wife shouldn't stand in his way. (Mine makes a mean breakfast, incidentally: scrambled eggs, hash brown potatoes, buttermilk biscuits, and a heaping mound of thick cut, maple flavor bacon!)

Even if you don't cook *all* the meals that you and your husband share, I recommend that you learn to cook at least a few things well. If he has a favorite dish, why not start with that?

There is something nice about preparing food for someone you love— something intimate about investing the time and energy necessary to whip up a delicious, nutritious meal for the man you married, even if you don't happen to share similar tastes.

> "Sharing food with another human being is an intimate act that should not be indulged in lightly."
>
> - M. F. K. Fisher

I have read that Ree Drummond (a.k.a. the Pioneer Woman) would prefer to live on sushi, sushi, and more sushi, but she married a meat-and-potatoes man.

So what do you think she did?

She learned how to prepare chicken fried steak and creamy mashed potatoes like a pro—and *became* a pro in the process. Now she's a wildly successful blogger, a New York Times #1 bestselling author, a popular television personality, and an award-winning photographer. God has blessed her phenomenally, and it all started with an earnest desire to please her man by feeding him his favorites.

God will bless you, too, when you make it a priority to serve things your husband likes. Results may vary: I can't promise you legions of devoted followers or a six-figure advance on your first cookbook, but I can guarantee you'll get a big "thumbs up" from the fans who matter most.

A happy hubby is just one of myriad blessings we glean by making meals our family looks forward to feasting upon. Studies have shown that the family dinner hour is also of vital importance to the health and wellbeing of children, so the more we can do to protect and preserve that time together, the better.[1]

> "Eating without conversation is only stoking."
>
> - Marcelene Cox

When it comes to memorable meals, the cuisine is only part of the equation. Ambiance and atmosphere deserve some special attention, as well.

This is not to imply that every meal must be served by candlelight using fine china—my own family eats more than its fair share of dinners off paper plates at a picnic table at the neighborhood pool—but some thought should be given to conversation and mood if we hope to satisfy our family's souls at the same time we fill their stomachs, for as Scripture reminds us:

- *"Better a dry crust with peace and quiet than a house full of feasting, with strife."*
  (Proverbs 17:1)
- *"Better is a dish of vegetables where love is than a fattened ox served with hatred."*
  (Proverbs 15:17)

## Chapter 13 – Feed Him His Favorites

- *"Man shall not live by bread alone but by every word that proceeds out of the mouth of God."* (Matthew 4:4)

Wholesome, delicious, nutritious food, served with love, seasoned with grace, blessed by God, and enjoyed with lively, uplifting conversation—that's my goal. Some meals fall short, but I'm pressing on. Won't you join me?

## Put It into Practice:

✎ Make a list of your husband's favorite foods. (If you don't already know, ask!) Then do your very best to incorporate as many as practical into your weekly meal plans.

✎ Jean de La Fontaine once wrote, "A hungry stomach cannot hear." If there is a topic of concern you need to discuss with your husband, try not to tackle it on an empty stomach. Feed him well. Let him unwind. Engage in pleasant conversation over the dinner table. Once his hunger has been addressed, then bring up the concern and work together toward a solution.

✎ If you have children, involve them in your meal preparations, too. Whenever you can, include their favorite dishes on the menu. Little ones especially love to help, and if you encourage that desire while they are young, they will be better equipped to prepare meals for themselves and/or their own families when the time comes for them to move away. I keep multiple copies of some kitchen tools, like potato peelers and cutting boards, so that my children can help without slowing me down. Over time, they'll get more proficient and may even surpass your culinary skills and abilities. (This is experience talking, as several of my own children are better cooks than I am at this point.)

Cherish
Togetherness

# Chapter 14

The day I first met my husband, we spent three hours so totally absorbed in conversation that we were oblivious to all else. A casual observer might have assumed we were just *talking*, but Doug was actually and actively sweeping me off my feet at the time.

"So... I heard you don't date," he said to me on our second meeting.

He'd heard right, although this was more a statement of fact than a matter of principle. At our small Christian college, everyone who knew me knew that I wanted to get married, have a lot of children, and home school them all—and there wasn't exactly a glut of guys vying for the chance to make that dream come true. The few who *had* ventured to ask me out had been summarily turned down (or scared off) once it became apparent that we didn't share the same vision or values.

But this guy was different. My life goals neither deterred nor intimidated him, but seemed rather to pique his interest.

"I don't date either," he continued. (By this he meant that he'd given up dating the minute he met me.) "So... how will we spend time together?"

He then proceeded to offer a slew of suggestions: Could we eat together in the cafeteria? *Yes.* Could we study together at the library? *Yes.* Could we go to church together on Sundays? *Yes.* Could we attend concerts, banquets, and other campus events together? *Yes. Yes. And yes, again.*

> "Coming together is a beginning.
> Keeping together is progress.
> Working together is success."
>
> - Henry Ford

The two of us have been virtually inseparable ever since. While we never did call it *dating*, we spent as many of our waking hours together as possible, then married a year later, so we could spend our resting hours together, as well.

Whether a couple is just starting out or has been married for years, togetherness is of vital importance for the nurture and health of their relationship. How can you truly know another person unless you spend time in his presence?

*80*

# Chapter 14 - Cherish Togetherness

Written letters, phone calls, texts, Skype, Twitter, Facebook—these are all great ways to stay connected when separation is unavoidable, but they can't hold a candle to communicating face to face with your beloved in the living, breathing flesh.

Some couples assume *togetherness* will be the status quo after marriage. They expect that if two people live under the same roof, they'll no longer have to work at coordinating schedules and carving out time for one another. That sort of thing just happens automatically, doesn't it?

Or does it?

That might be true for the time a couple is on their honeymoon trip, but as soon as they get back home and return to school or work, life's other obligations and responsibilities will begin

> "I think togetherness is a very important ingredient to family life."
>
> - Barbara Bush

conspiring to distract their attention, steal their time, and dampen their intimacy. Unless husband and wife are both careful to protect, preserve, and cherish their time together, it will slowly be eroded away and their relationship will suffer as a result.

To keep that from happening, you must be intentional about the time you spend with your spouse. Don't let outside activities infringe upon your time together as a couple. You may have no choice but to be apart during working hours, but limit extra-curricular activities that segregate you from one another too frequently.

Given the choice, many men prefer to communicate shoulder-to-shoulder rather than face-to-face.[1] They like to be actively involved in *doing* something and get a bit antsy when we try to make them sit still and *talk* for hours on end.

If your husband falls into such a category, then adapt yourself to that mindset. Either do things with him, or be an enthusiastic observer when he does them, even if that just means sitting nearby as he tinkers on the car or cheering him on as he shoots baskets in the driveway.

> "Love endures only when the lovers love many things together and not merely each other."
>
> - Walter Lippmann

I love being close to my husband, even when we aren't talking to one another.

Our church shares a potluck meal every Sunday afternoon, and although the men and women normally sit separately to visit over lunch, I always position myself close enough to my husband that I can listen to his conversations, too, as I think everything he says is so interesting.

At home, I'll take my book or handwork to whatever room in the house he's working in, just to be close to him, because I enjoy his company, even when neither of us has anything to say (admittedly rare—but it does happen). Togetherness doesn't have to involve talking at all. Seek out your husband's company and cherish the time you get to spend together. Don't ever take that time for granted, but be grateful for it and recognize it for the blessing it is.

## Put It into Practice:

✍ Set time aside daily to connect with your husband. Maybe over coffee in the morning before kids are up and work duties call, or maybe over a warm bath in the evening before you turn in at night. Either way, use the time as an opportunity to discuss the day's events and your thoughts concerning them, to relate funny or interesting things that happened while your were apart, to summarize the day's accomplishments, to share any concerns, needs, or prayer requests, and to pray about them together.

✍ Jealously guard your family time in the evenings. As much as possible, say no to evening activities that take you and your husband in separate directions. An occasional board meeting or girls night out may be fine, but when your family is fragmented every night of the week for months on end, it undermines all sense of togetherness.

✍ If you still haven't installed a dependable lock on your bedroom door, please do not wait another day to do so. This will afford you and your husband instant privacy whenever you want or need it, which is especially important once children join the family.

✍ Take an active interest in your husband's hobbies. Learn what you can about his favorite sports and pastimes, then join him as a fan, a cheerleader, or an active participant.

Don't
Complain

## Chapter 15

The Bible says we should "do everything without complaining or arguing." (Philippians 2:14, NLT)

That's not a suggestion. It's a command.

Nobody wants to be around a whiner or complainer. It is wearisome, both mentally and emotionally, to listen to the constant grumblings of a perpetually unhappy person. It grates on the nerves.

Wise parents understand this fact and train their children to communicate without whining. Our Heavenly Father expects no less from us, as is repeatedly made clear in Scripture:

- *"Jesus answered and said to them, 'Do not grumble among yourselves.'"* (John 6:43)
- *"Do not complain, brethren, against one another so that you yourselves may not be judged; behold, the Judge is standing right at the door."* (James 5:9)
- *"How long shall I bear with this evil congregation who are grumbling against Me? I have heard the complaints of the sons of Israel, which they are making against Me."* (Numbers 14:27)
- *"And don't grumble as some of them did, and then were destroyed by the angel of death."* (1 Corinthians 10:10)

These last two references demonstrate how strongly the Lord dislikes murmuring and complaining.

> "We can complain because rose bushes have thorns, or rejoice because thorn bushes have roses."
>
> - Abraham Lincoln

Whenever the children of Israel chose grumbling over gratefulness, they were chastised severely.

Although it's true God encourages us to make all our requests known unto Him, He clearly desires that we do so with a spirit of gratitude, humility, and respect—rather than with an attitude of pride, bitterness, or entitlement.

The following verses bear this out:

- *"...but in everything by prayer and supplication **with thanksgiving** let your requests be made known to God."* (Philippians 4:6)
- *"Devote yourselves to prayer, being watchful **and thankful."** (Colossians 4:2, NIV)
- *"Pray without ceasing; in everything **give thanks**; for this is God's will for you in Christ Jesus."* (1 Thessalonians 5:17-18)

When I say that a wife shouldn't complain, I don't mean she should never appeal for her husband's help with problems or talk to him about issues that weigh heavily on her mind. Rather, I'm simply suggesting that she examine her heart before beginning such a discussion or making such an appeal, to be certain she is doing so in an appreciative, humble, and respectful manner. The proper attitude goes a long way toward eliciting a positive response.

> "Had we not faults of our own, we should take less pleasure in complaining of others."
>
> - François Fénelon

Not only should a wife avoid complaining *to* her husband, but she must also resist the urge to complain *about* him, for the second habit is even more dishonoring than the first.

Years ago, I joined a group of relatively young wives for a lunch I'll not soon forget, for it quickly evolved into a gripe session where each participant launched into a detailed description of some stupid thing her husband had recently done. No sooner did one finish speaking than the next tried to outdo her. To hear them talk, you would think they had all married a bunch of imbeciles, although I can assure you this was not the case.

I had absolutely no desire to join in this discussion. In fact, I felt guilty for even being privy to the conversation, which centered on mostly minor offenses: some purchase the wife deemed frivolous or a bungled household repair. It wasn't even so much what they said, but the way they said it.[1]

> "It is not so much the greatness of our troubles, as the littleness of our spirit, which makes us complain."
>
> - Hudson Taylor

It's not that I think my husband is perfect.[2] He makes his fair share of mistakes (just as I do), but that has never been my focus. I sometimes say or do dumb things, too, but I'd be mortified to think he was sharing the details of all my flubs with his friends or coworkers in a disgusted, derisive way. And I know that little group of girlfriends would've likewise been humiliated, were the tables turned on them. Whatever happened to, *"Treat others as you yourself would like to be treated"?*[3]

Again, it all boils down to focus. Are you going to center your thoughts on what is wrong with the world, wrong with your husband, wrong with your home? Or will you choose to look at things with eyes of gratitude, love, and respect?

There are countless things in life over which we have no control, but we can control our thoughts and attitudes and responses. So let's begin there.

## Put It into Practice:

✍ Keep a mental tally for a few days of the positive things you say to your husband over any negatives you mention. See how big you can make that ratio.

✍ Make prayer your first response, not your last resort. Next time you're tempted to complain about anything to your spouse, pray about it first. Remember the serenity prayer: accept the things you can't change, change the things you can, seek wisdom to know the difference.[4]

✍ When discussing problems with your husband, keep your communication clear, concise, and respectful: "The pipe under the sink is leaking. Should I call a plumber, or do you think we can fix it ourselves?" Resist the temptation to drone on and on about minor annoyances. Address them quickly and move on.

✍ I received a letter from one disgruntled [ex]wife whose "honey-do list" had grown to five typewritten, single-spaced pages. She felt that the divorce was all her husband's fault for not tending to her list in a timely fashion. Please don't let broken hinges and leaky faucets destroy your marriage, if home repairs aren't your husband's forte. Get a good book on household repairs and learn to fix things yourself. It really isn't that difficult and will save both you and your husband a lot of frustration.

Resist the Urge
to Correct

# Chapter 16

In the early days of our marriage, I would occasionally try to edit my husband's stories as he told them. I guess I thought my duties as a helpmeet included fact-checking every statement my spouse ever made for accuracy. Since he is very detail oriented himself, I thought he'd appreciate my contribution in this area.

I was wrong.[1]

Nobody likes to be contradicted, but men—I have since come to realize—especially abhor it.

Guys crave respect. A man wants to be perceived by others as being knowledgeable and authoritative—yet that's virtually impossible if the missus makes a habit of challenging every word out of his mouth.

I know one fellow who can't tell a simple story without his wife stopping him fifteen times to correct some inconsequential detail: "It wasn't Monday *morning,* it was Monday *afternoon...* I wouldn't call it *blue*, it was more of a *turquoise....* We didn't ride the *bus*, we took a *taxi.*"

Please. Please. *Please.* Don't do that to your husband—or to anyone else, for that matter!

It makes a man feel foolish to have the things he says called into question. If it happens repeatedly, he may become emotionally withdrawn and stop communicating altogether, rather than be forced to argue with his wife over each and every little point.

> "Correction does much, but encouragement does more."
>
> - Johann Wolfgang von Goethe

Of course, everyone makes mistakes. So what's a wife to do when she hears her husband misspeak in her presence?

That's something each couple must work out on their own, but here are a few rules of thumb I've learned over the years that have helped keep me out of trouble:

- If my husband speaks in error, but it is not a critical mistake—say he tells a friend he caught a 12-pound catfish, but I distinctly remember it was only 11½—then I just let it slide.[2] There's no sense interrupting a good story to clarify something that doesn't make any difference.

- If my husband makes a mistake that may cause problems down the line for somebody else—like he tells a friend to turn right when he really needs to turn left[3]—then I try to amend the information in as gentle a manner as possible. One good way to do this is by asking a question, "Did you mean for him to turn right at that light or left?" This keeps me from looking pushy or stupid when my husband goes on to explain, "Yeah, there was a break in the water main and the road he'd normally take is closed for repairs, so he'll have to go the long way around." Remember that your husband may have information to which you aren't privy, so never use a know-it-all tone with him.[4]

- Occasionally my husband will look to me for help when he's unsure of some pertinent piece of information: "Now correct me if I'm wrong, but I think that so-in-so does such-in-such." In such cases, I try to come to his aid as quickly as possible, even if it means just pulling out my iPhone and turfing the question to Siri.

- My husband has a phenomenal memory—except when it comes to names. And thanks to a handful of past embarrassing mistakes, he sometimes hesitates to use the names he *does* remember. So when the two of us run into somebody we both know, I try to drop that person's name immediately so Doug will be able to use it, too. If we meet someone who obviously knows my husband, but Doug stalls for even a moment in introducing that person to me, I quickly extend my hand and introduce myself. The person will normally supply his own name in return, so that way we all know it.

These above guidelines are helpful when your husband misspeaks, but perhaps you're thinking it's not his words that need correcting, so much as his behavior.

What then?

Well, if the bothersome behavior is immoral, illegal, or endangering your family, then you may need to enlist the help of a trained professional in order to establish some accountability.

But if you're just peeved because your guy keeps leaving the toilet seat up or throwing his dirty socks on the floor, you should do your best to get over it.

After all, your husband could be just as easily annoyed with you for leaving the seat *down* or for hiding his socks in the laundry hamper when he was planning to re-wear them.

> "Criticism, like rain, should be gentle enough to nourish a man's growth without destroying his roots."
>
> - Frank A. Clark

## Chapter 16 - Resist the Urge to Correct

If you really want to transform your marriage, use each little irritation or annoyance as a signal to pray for your husband and for your marriage. Pray that God would give you patience and understanding and grace and *gratitude*.

Again, gratitude is key.

When you find the toilet seat up? Thank God. Thank Him that you have indoor plumbing and a seat to leave up. Thank Him that you have a roof over your head and a husband (albeit a forgetful one). Thank Him that your husband can walk to the bathroom and stand over the toilet unassisted. Thank Him that you have eyes to notice when the seat's left up and hands to lower it back into place.

Alternatively, thank Him that you didn't break your neck when you fell in!

> "Thank the Lord for using each person as a tool in your life to deepen your insight into His grace and for conforming you to the image of His Son."
>
> - Charles Stanley

I should probably clarify, for the record, that my own husband is very thoughtful in both these areas. He never leaves the seat up, nor does he throw smelly socks on the floor.

In fact, as soon as he pulls a pair of socks off his feet, he turns them right side out, smoothes them flat, lines up their edges, and lays them neatly in our laundry hamper atop all his other carefully folded dirty clothes.

It's an endearing practice, to be sure, but not one he learned from me (nor passed on to our progeny)!

Of course, my husband also loves to cart stuff off to Goodwill without warning, so he isn't *completely* devoid of annoying habits.[5] I get plenty of opportunities to practice what I preach by showing grace to my man.

> "No, you're not allowed to be bossy when you're married. You have to learn compromise, and compassion, and patience."
>
> - Star Jones

And, although I do my best to minimize it, he gets quite a few chances to exercise grace toward me, as well—like when I throw my inside-out, wadded up laundry on top of his meticulously stacked and folded dirty clothes. Or when I try to lecture him about what he shouldn't have sent to Goodwill! Hence, this chapter on resisting the urge to correct serves as much as a reminder to myself as to anybody else.

## Put It into Practice:

✍ What triggers you to climb on a soapbox? Identify the kinds of statements or behaviors that launch you into lecture mode, then think through your reaction beforehand. If the issue is not really that important, let it go. If you feel strongly that it is an issue that needs to be addressed, then speak to your husband privately and calmly about the matter, after the heat of the moment has passed.

✍ A thoughtful wife will do what she can to make her husband look good. If he needs help with something (like a forgotten name), come to his aid in as discreet a manner as possible. After all, his reputation is your reputation.

✍ It's especially important to present a united front when it comes to rearing children. Be supportive of your husband, even if he doesn't always do things exactly as you think they should be done.[6] I'm grateful to have realized early on that my angry, disapproving, or controlling attitude toward my husband would in the long run do much more damage to my children than the sweet iced tea, the rough and tumble play, the burp-talking, or the eighty's music to which I was so prone to object.

Dress to
Please Him

# Chapter 17

When I first published an abbreviated version of *25 Ways to Communicate Respect* on my Loving Life at Home blog back in August of 2012, I was astounded to see how many women took offense at my suggestion that a wife should dress in a way her husband finds attractive.

In my mind, there were points on the list that were far more controversial than this one—I *expected those* might draw some criticism—but I never imagined #17 would provoke the ire of so many readers.

No, I'm not trying to reduce women to the sum of their physical attributes, as some falsely accuse. I concede that a woman's worth is based on infinitely more than what she looks like.

But to say that our appearance does not matter *most* is not to imply that it does not matter *at all.* Men are visual creatures. Putting a wedding ring on their finger does not negate that fact.

Many of us went to great lengths to look good *before* we got married. We combed and curled and coiffed our hair. We slicked on lip-gloss and crimped our eyelashes and primped in front of the mirror for hours on end.

Why? Because we wanted to look our best. We were trying to attract our guy's attention. We were willing to do whatever it took to snag a husband and make him our own.

Is it fair, then, for us to pull a bait-and-switch after the wedding? Promising an attractive, pulled-together wife, but delivering curlers and cold cream?

Why do we seem to think that once we marry, we can stop *trying?*

There may be little chance that I'll ever be mistaken for a trophy wife, but do I really want to present myself in a way that removes all doubt? After all, the Bible does say that a virtuous wife is a crown to her husband. (Proverbs 12:4) Isn't a crown a little bit like a trophy?

> "Adornment is never anything except a reflection of the heart."
>
> - Gabrielle "Coco" Chanel

# Chapter 17 - Dress to Please Him

I want my man to be proud to show me off in public. Don't you? Don't you want to keep your spouse captivated?

Then dress the part.

This doesn't mean you have to clean your house in a cocktail dress and stiletto heels or shop for groceries in revealing negligees, nor do you need to wear things that you detest or find uncomfortable, but I do think you should take care of your appearance and dress in a way that pleases the man you married.

Notice I say you should wear what *your* husband finds attractive. Not what *my husband* thinks is attractive. Not what your mother says is attractive. Not what your girlfriends tell you is attractive. Not what the fashion industry passes off as attractive.

- My mother thinks I look my best when I'm wearing a little lipstick and mascara, but my husband hates lipstick and mascara, so I normally go barefaced. (That way he can kiss me whenever he wants without worrying about color transfer or collar stains.)
- Fashion rules say that redheads shouldn't wear red, but I love wearing red, and my husband thinks I look terrific wearing red, so I wear red all the time.
- My girlfriends look great sporting bobbed hair and pixie cuts, but my husband likes for me to wear my hair long, so long it is.[1]

Of course, you can't take your spouse's preferences into account if you're not sure what those preferences are, so if you don't know, ask. Does he like for you to wear things that are tailored or frilly? Fitted or flowing? What colors does he think look best on you? What hairstyle? Does he like you to wear make-up? Jewelry? Perfume?

If you can't ask him these questions (or if he refuses to answer them for fear of hurting your feelings), then experiment a little and watch his reactions. Which of your outfits elicit the most compliments? Which make him really sit up and take notice?

> "Fashions fade, style is eternal."
>
> - Yves Saint Laurent

When you find something he seems to like, stock up on things in the same style or color.

You don't need to consult your spouse every time you want to change clothes—just fill your closet with clothes he favors, and you'll be good to go, whatever you choose to wear.

Women in the work force often adhere to very strict standards of dress, whether written or unwritten. You don't see many female executives showing up at the office in their bathrobes and slippers, do you? Lots of women—including surgeons, waitresses, nurses, police officers, and even Supreme Court justices—must wear prescribed uniforms to work every day.

So why all the resistance about looking good on the home front?

There is nothing demeaning about a woman wearing clothes her husband finds flattering and pretty. This is not oppressive. It's not objectification.[2]

It is simply something a wife chooses to do because she loves her man and values his opinions. It's the same reason she pays attention to her health and hygiene and tries to get adequate rest and exercise—not only because she respects husband, but because she respects herself and wants to look and feel her best.

- She wants to look her best in public, because she understands that when she goes out into the community, she is not only representing herself, but her husband and family, as well.
- She wants to look her best at home, because she knows that looking good and feeling comfortable does not have to be an either-or proposition. (And she can really rock an apron).
- She wants to look her best in private, because that's when it's especially easy to please her guy. (Just because an outfit is not modest enough to wear in public

> "Of all the things you wear, your expression is the most important."
>
> - Janet Lane

or in front of the kids does not mean you can never wear it at all. Lock the bedroom door and slip into something just for your husband. Do this regularly enough, and he won't care what you wear to clean out the garage.)

Do keep in mind that looking our best encompasses much more than what clothes we put on our bodies. Our appearance is more than our apparel.

Scripture tells us our "*adornment must not be merely external—braiding the hair, and wearing gold jewelry, or putting on dresses; but it [should] be the hidden person of the heart, with the imperishable quality of a gentle and quiet spirit, which is precious in the sight of God."* (1 Peter 3:3-4)

So our carriage also comes into play. Our attitudes and deportment speak volumes, revealing not only what we think of ourselves, but also how we regard those around us.

Including our husbands.

"What attracts men to women is their femininity," writes radio personality Laura Schlessinger, "and femininity isn't only about appearance, it's also about behaviors. Looking womanly and behaving sweetly and flirtatiously are gifts wives give to their husbands. This gift communicates that the husband is seen as a man, not just a fix-it guy, the bread-winner, or the sperm donor."[3]

"You're never fully dressed without a smile."

- Martin Charnin

That is a great reminder. Sprucing up for your husband and treating him like a man is not only good for him and good for your marriage—it's good for you, as well. Doesn't it make you feel strong and confident and desirable when you flash your husband a knowing smile and his heart gives a little flutter in response? You captivated his attention *before* marriage. Why not make an effort to turn his head again?

## Put It into Practice:

- ✍ Think back to when you were first getting to know this man you married. What was it that first attracted his attention to you? Do your best to play up that feature once again.

- ✍ Ask your husband to go through your closet and remove any clothes that he does not like to see you wear or doesn't feel are flattering to you.

- ✍ If there's a particular color or style that your husband likes to see you wear, stock up on clothes that fit that description.

- ✍ Invest in some beautiful lingerie to wear when you are alone with your husband. Be playful and girlie. Give him a feast for his eyes.

Keep the
House Tidy

## Chapter 18

To the best of your abilities, try to maintain a clean and orderly home. "A man's house is his castle," as the saying goes, so seek to make it a haven of rest for your entire family, a place your husband will look forward to returning at the end of a long day.

I'm not trying to chain anybody to a vacuum cleaner here. And I understand that when both husband and wife work outside the home, chores may need to be split up a little differently than when one spouse is at home all day. But whether we are fulltime homemakers or not, we would do well to follow the Proverbs 31 wife's example, who diligently *"watches over the affairs of her household"* and refuses to *"eat the bread of idleness."* (Proverbs 31:27)

Whatever chores we do, whether the lion's share or an even split with our spouse, should be done consistently, cheerfully, and as unto the Lord. Although our families certainly benefit when we keep a tidy home, our faithfulness in this area is ultimately a service to God (Ephesians 6:7; Colossians 3:23).

He holds us accountable for everything entrusted to our care (including our home), and He expects us to use it in a way that blesses those around us and glorifies Him.

> "Housework is what a woman does that nobody notices unless she hasn't done it."
>
> - Evan Esar

God is *not* the author of chaos and confusion, so messes and mayhem should *not* be the pattern for our homes.

Rather, He is a God of order. He has set the stars in their places and has numbered the hairs on our heads. He's established the season, so that spring always follows winter and summer always follows spring—right on schedule, never fail. We can count on it.

That is one of the many benefits to running an orderly and well-scheduled household—it lets your family know what to expect and gives your life together a comforting, reassuring rhythm. Since God created us in His own image, we should make it our goal to reflect this orderly aspect of His character.

# Chapter 18 - Keep the House Tidy

There are several habits that almost all good housekeepers have in common:

**First, a good housekeeper has a reliable method for dealing with clutter**. Rather than letting junk mail pile up on her desk or kitchen counter for days or weeks at a time, she tosses it straight in the trash or recycle bin as soon as it enters the house.

She deals with broken toys, outgrown clothes, leftover food, and anything else that has outlived its usefulness in similar fashion, purging her home of worthless junk and keeping everything in it in good working order.

> "Run a home like you would a small business and treat it with the same seriousness."
>
> - Anthea Turner

**Second, a good housekeeper designates a place for everything and keeps everything in place.** She rarely needs to spend precious minutes hunting car keys or purses or shoes when she's in a hurry to go somewhere, because each of those items can be found exactly where it belongs.[1]

She stores the most frequently used items in the most easily accessible space, making it a simple matter to return anything to its proper home. She also stores things as near their point of use as possible (coffee mugs and creamer close to the coffee maker, garbage bags and dust pan beside the trash can, copy paper and computer ink next to the printer, etc.).

**Third, a good housekeeper is a good problem solver.** She's not afraid to think outside the box. If one approach isn't working, she's not afraid to try another.

If dirty shoes keep tracking mud onto clean floors, she'll put a shelf or basket by the door so kids can shed their shoes before coming inside. If the clothes rod in the coat closet is too high for her little ones to reach, she'll install hooks at their level so they can hang up their jackets that way instead of dropping them on the floor.

**Fourth, a good housekeeper routinely enlists the help of others.** She realizes she cannot do everything herself. This is especially important when children are part of the picture.

The greater the number of children in a household, the more frazzled the homemaker will become unless those children are trained to pitch in and help. Where there are no oxen, the stable stays clean (Proverbs 14:4). And where there are no kids, the house stays straight. But both cattle and children enrich our lives in ways that make keeping them around well worth the hassle.

> "Cleaning your house while your kids are still growing is like shoveling the sidewalk before it stops snowing."
>
> - Phyllis Diller

Some mess is to be expected when sharing a home with little ones, but if you are always inside the house working while your children are outside playing, then something is amiss.

# Chapter 18 - Keep the House Tidy

I know, I know. It often seems easier to do the chores yourself without little ones under foot, but the cost of this perceived convenience is too high: Not only are you missing out on the opportunity to make precious memories with them, both at work and at play, but you are forfeiting an opportunity to teach them important life skills.

When everyone pitches in to get the work done, the chores are (theoretically) finished faster, and then you can all relax and have fun together as a family.

**Fifth and finally, a good housekeeper makes wise use of whatever time is available.** She doesn't wait until she has a full day to devote to house cleaning to get started. She realizes that little by little will add up over time.

She also recognizes the value of a job half-done. If she doesn't have time to deep clean, she spot cleans. If she doesn't have time to spot clean, she straightens.

> "Housework can kill you if done right."
>
> - Erma Bombeck

She knows no matter how thoroughly she scours a cluttered house—washing windows and vacuuming rugs and polishing doorknobs—it will still *seem* dirty if the beds aren't made or there's paper strewn all over the floor.

Conversely, she understands that an uncluttered house, one where everything's picked up and put away, will *look* clean, even if the furniture still needs dusting or the floor hasn't been swept.

Here, as in so many other things, there is a need for balance. Keeping a tidy house should be a means to an end, not the end goal itself.

I view housekeeping as a way to serve God by being a good steward over what He has given me, to care for my family by creating a pleasant place for us all to live, to show gratitude to my husband for the home he has provided, to honor him by keeping it neat and clean the way he likes it, to train my children to be conscientious and competent workers, and to reach out to others by extending hospitality.

> "Love begins at home, and it is not how much we do... but how much love we put in that action."
>
> - Mother Teresa

If my desire for a clean house makes me irritable and impatient with the people inside it, then my priorities are misplaced. If I go berserk when a child spills milk on my freshly mopped floor, instead of gently coming alongside to assist and instruct in wiping up the mess, then my clean house has become an idol, and I'm sending my family the message that it is more important to me than they are.

Keeping an immaculate house (in the strictest sense of the word) is not really possible this side of heaven, so it's futile to make that our goal.

Keeping a tidy house, on the other hand, is entirely achievable—even while maintaining a proper and loving attitude toward everyone who lives there.

## Put It into Practice:

✎ Think about which things are most prone to go missing-in-action at your house. Shoes? Scissors? Cell phones? Whatever they are, assign a logical home to each object once and for all, then force yourself (and remind others) to return these items to their proper place every time they're used.

✎ Don't wait until your place looks perfect before inviting company over. Instead, make a date *now* to have some friends over within the next two weeks, then use the upcoming visit as motivation to complete a few neglected chores before they arrive. If you don't get everything done? Don't worry. After all, you're friends aren't coming to see your house, they're coming to see *you.*

✎ Multi-task when possible. Fold a load of laundry or clean out a drawer while you're stuck on the phone. Clean as you go when cooking, as well, emptying the dishwasher while you wait for water to boil or wiping down counters while the soup is simmering.

✎ Don't get too fixated on traditional gender roles when it comes to chores. You don't have to have a Y-chromosome to fix a leaky faucet or operate a lawnmower. I have a girlfriend, in fact, who claims mowing the lawn is her *favorite* job. "It's the only chore I do," she says, "that I know will *stay* done for an entire week!"

Be Content

## Chapter 19

Dale Carnegie once said, "It isn't what you have or who you are or where you are or what you are doing that makes you happy or unhappy. It is what you think about it."[1]

Contentment is the same way.

It doesn't really matter how much you have or how nice it is or how it compares to what your neighbor's got (or how long it's going to take to pay it off!). What counts is how you feel about those things.

If you spend more time worrying about what you lack instead of being thankful for what you have, then you do not know the true meaning of contentment.

Contentment is not the same thing as complacency. It is something different than apathy. It doesn't mean you give up, quit trying, or stop reaching toward new goals.

> "He who is not contented with what he has, would not be contented with what he would like to have."
>
> - Socrates

Rather, contentment means accepting your present circumstances for what they are and endeavoring to learn what you can in the midst of them. It means recognizing and being grateful for every blessing.

Contentment means remembering that the same God who began a good work in you will be faithful to complete it. (Philippians 1:6; 1 Thessalonians 5:24) It means finding your satisfaction in the Savior. The Bible has much to say regarding this kind of contentment:

- *"I have learned to be content in whatever circumstances I am. I know how to get along with humble means, and I also know how to live in prosperity; in any and every circumstance I have learned the secret of being filled and going hungry, both of having abundance and suffering need. I can do all*

*116*

*things through Him who strengthens me."* (Philippians 4:11-13)

- *"But godliness with contentment is great gain. For we brought nothing into the world, and we can take nothing out of it. But if we have food and clothing, we will be content with that."* (1 Timothy 6:6-8, NIV)

- *"Don't love money; be satisfied with what you have. For God has said, 'I will never fail you. I will never abandon you.'"* (Hebrews 13:5, NLT)

- *"The fear of the LORD leads to life; then one rests content, untouched by trouble."* (Proverbs 19:23, NIV)

"Be thankful for what you have; you'll end up having more. If you concentrate on what you don't have, you will never, ever have enough"

- Oprah Winfrey

- *"For this reason I say to you, do not be worried about your life, as to what you will eat or what you will drink; nor for your body, as to what you will put on. Is not life more than food, and the body more than clothing? But seek first His kingdom and His righteousness, and all these things will be added to you."* (Matthew 6:25, 33)

Do you want to communicate respect to your husband? Then don't make him feel like he has to keep up with the Joneses to make you happy. Take satisfaction in the lifestyle he is able to provide for you, and find hope in the future the two of you are seeking to build together.

> "Do not spoil what you have by desiring what you have not."
>
> - Ann Brashares

Financial strain can be deadly to a marriage, regardless of which spouse is bringing home the paycheck, so always be careful to live within your means. Don't let money issues divide you. Instead, use lean times as an opportunity to pull together, to buckle down, to exercise resourcefulness, and to think creatively through ways you might better your circumstances.

Each hardship you face as a couple can serve to further cement your love and appreciation for one another, if only you'll keep counting your blessings and working as a team to meet the challenges life brings your way, content that God has a purpose and a plan for every one of them.

## Put It into Practice:

🖑 What are the things you are most inclined to worry about? Make a list and lay it at the feet of Jesus. Ask God to open your eyes to what He wants you to learn in the midst of these trials.

🖑 A wise person once observed, "Contentment isn't about having what you want, but about wanting what you have." Whenever you feel like focusing on all the things you *don't* have, review the "Blessings Journal" you started in chapter 1, and thank God again for all those things you *do* have.

🖑 Do you ever engage in "retail therapy"? If you are a person who buys stuff as a way to address some deep longing in your soul, realize that the emptiness you are feeling won't ever be satisfied with material things. Next time you are tempted to whip out your credit card and purchase something you don't need, step away from the cash register. Use the same trigger that leads you to impulse shop as a prompt to read your Bible or to identify and donate to charity something you own but don't use.

🖑 If there is something you truly need but can't afford, pray to God about it. He promises to supply all our needs "according to His riches in glory in Christ Jesus." (Philippians 4:19) In the meantime, work hard, save up, and ask God to bless your efforts.

Take
His Advice

## Chapter 20

Do not dismiss your husband's opinions lightly, especially when you've asked for his counsel in the first place. Make every effort to follow his advice.

"But I *didn't ask* for any advice," many wives object. "I was just telling a story."

A woman will often get perturbed when her husband launches into fix-it mode instead of simply providing a sympathetic ear when she needs it. When she's upset about something, she interprets this hasty rush to a solution as evidence that her husband doesn't really understand the situation, doesn't fully appreciate the distress it has caused her, can't adequately *feel* her pain. She may even think that his no-nonsense approach to the matter is just an attempt to shut her up, because he's tired of hearing her bellyache.

I've entertained such thoughts myself in the past, and still have a hard time believing they aren't at least partially true.

"Many receive advice, only the wise profit from it."

- Harper Lee

Yet, according to a growing body of scientific evidence, our husbands respond the way they do simply because that is how their brains are wired.[1] Studies have now confirmed what we've all long suspected: Men and women think very differently.

A man can't understand why his wife would waste valuable time complaining about something he could easily fix in just a few minutes. And a woman is equally perplexed, because her husband seems incapable of listening without taking on an advisory role.[2]

Often, all we really want is a little sympathy.

We have to realize, however, that this *is* a husband's way of sympathizing. It causes him distress to see his wife in pain.[3] Mentally searching for a solution is his way of communicating that distress, of proving to her he cares, of expressing heartfelt empathy in the way that comes most naturally to him.

Even so, it grates on us. So what's a beleaguered wife to do?

If you want to avoid the conflict that sometimes springs from your spouse's different method of thinking about and dealing with problems, then you really have only three options:

1. Stop complaining
2. Warn him ahead of time if all you want is a hug or a prayer or a shoulder to cry on
3. Listen to his counsel and accept his advice

We've already discussed the first option at length in Chapter 15, so I won't rehash all that here.

The second option may (theoretically) help from a wife's point of view, but I imagine it will feel like torture to her husband.

> "Advice is what we ask for when we already know the answer but wish we didn't."
>
> - Erica Jong

Consider how you would react if the tables were turned: Imagine that your husband has come home complaining of feeling famished. You offer him a snack, try to cook him some dinner, point him to the pantry, propose going out to eat, but your every suggestion is met with fierce resistance. Not only that, but your spouse accuses you of being insensitive for even attempting to come up with a solution.

"Why do you always have to *fix* things?" he might ask in exasperation. "I haven't eaten all day! I'm starting to feel faint! Can't you see how upset I am? I don't need advice; I need sympathy. I just want to know that you're on my side—that you understand!"

Wouldn't it feel a little disingenuous to merely pat your husband on the back in such a situation and tell him that you're sorry he's having such a hard time?

Well, that's exactly how our husbands feel, too, when we put such constraints on them and attempt to dictate their emotional responses. In the same way that you'd feel compelled to let your hungry husband know there's hot bread in the oven, your husband feels obligated to share his best answer to whatever problem is troubling *you*.

> "To profit from good advice requires more wisdom than to give it."
>
> - Wilson Mizner

Which brings us to the third option: Listen to your husband's counsel and accept his advice. Don't automatically pooh-pooh his suggestions. He's offering you a fresh perspective, a different vantage point, so hear him out, then do your best to implement his most reasonable recommendations.

Believe me, I know this is easier said than done. I do not like change in general, so my knee-jerk reaction to any suggestion that we do something differently is to argue in favor of the status quo.

This usually backfires.

That's because, in God's great providence, I married a man who embraces change with enthusiasm. You might even say he likes change for change's sake, although life with me has tempered that tendency somewhat. (Isn't it wonderful how God balances extremes in personalities by uniting them in holy matrimony?)

I've learned not to complain about trivial matters, because I know my doing so will trigger my husband's problem-solving circuits, which will inevitably lead to some sort of change that feels (to me) like more of a hassle than whatever matter I was grousing about to begin with.

Unfortunately, this does not get me completely off the hook in the advice department, because sometimes my spouse will simply *see* something he thinks is not working as well as it should and will make suggestions based on that observation.

> "It is very difficult to live among people you love and hold back from offering them advice."
>
> - Anne Tyler

My husband is very smart, extremely attentive to detail, and amazingly adept at "thinking outside the box."

So why wouldn't I want to immediately adopt whatever measure he's proposing? My inborn aversion to change is only part of the problem. If I'm honest, I must admit the rest of it stems from my *pride.*

The Bible tells us, "*Pride leads to conflict; those who take advice are wise.*" (Proverbs 13:10, NLT)

Ouch! Isn't that verse convicting? What makes me resistant to my husband's advice? What makes me want to argue about the best course of action?

The Bible says it's my pride. "Where there is strife, there is pride," is how the NIV translates it. Wherever strife and arguments and contention exist, we can be certain *pride* is somehow involved.

It boils down to this: I want my way. I'm convinced my way is better. Is it better? Maybe. Maybe not. I'll never know unless I hear my husband out. It is arrogant and stubborn and foolish for me to cling to my own way without even bothering to consider his ideas about a given matter.

> "Pride leads to conflict; those who take advice are wise."
>
> - Proverbs 13:10 (NLT)

His ideas are almost always reasonable. It would be fair to say that many of his ideas border on brilliant. We both know this, so it's insulting and hurtful to him when I blithely discount or dismiss his suggestions.

Taking my husband's advice does not mean I'm incapable of thinking through problems or coming up with solutions on my own. It just means I'm willing to consider his perspective and give his way a try.

Why not do the same at your house? Next time you face a problem, ask for your husband's advice and follow it.

Doing so does not make you weak.

It makes you smart.

## Put It into Practice:

- ✍ Next time your husband launches into fix-it mode, don't bristle. Take a deep breath and remind yourself that his brain is wired differently than yours. Listen to his suggestions and implement whichever seems most reasonable. Don't forget to thank him for his help!

- ✍ Don't wait for your husband to offer you advice. Ask for it! Pick some neutral decision you are currently facing—what to make for dinner tonight?—seek his counsel and run with it.

- ✍ Assume your husband's good intentions. Do not view his suggestions as an attempt to micromanage your life. Trust that he has the best interest of your entire family at heart, and respond in kind.

Admire
Him

# Chapter 21

Think back to what first attracted you to your husband. Chances are, at least a few of those traits are still there, so take time to notice and comment on them.

- Tuck little love notes into his briefcase, under his pillow, between the pages of a book he's reading.
- Commend him for his wisdom, patience, integrity, work ethic.
- Rave over his dashing good looks, his gorgeous eyes, his broad shoulders, his sexy legs.

- Text him to let him know you miss him and have something special planned for his homecoming.
- Compliment his most admirable qualities when speaking of him to others—especially when he can overhear your doing so.

Voiced compliments and heartfelt praise are always welcome, but you should also make it your habit to just look at your husband in a respectful, appreciative way. Think kind thoughts toward him. He'll be able to see the admiration in your eyes.

Plus, all those positive thoughts will spill over into your speech, for as Jesus told his disciples:

"To love is to admire with the heart; to admire is to love with the mind."

- Theophile Gautier

*A good person produces good things from the treasury of a good heart, and an evil person produces evil things from the treasury of an evil heart. What you say flows from what is in your heart.* (Luke 6:45, NLT)

Not only do our husbands want to be told we admire them, but they want to be told why. Nobody likes being taken for granted, so let him know you think he's awesome. Be as specific, as generous, and as sincere as you can with the compliments, and his appreciation for you will soar!

## Put It into Practice:

✍ Text your husband every day for a week, thanking him each day for a different character quality you admire.

✍ Read through Song of Solomon for some very creative word pictures expressing admiration for one's beloved. Use those as a model to write your husband a nice, long love letter of your own.

✍ Whenever somebody else says something nice about your husband, be sure to pass the compliment along to him and voice your agreement.

✍ Write a poem or compose a song, be it silly or serious, extolling your husband's many virtues, as well as his most impressive physical attributes. Share it with him when the time is right.

Guard His
Reputation

# Chapter 22

I am something of a legend at the hospital where my husband serves as Chief of Staff. Whenever he introduces me to anybody from work, I always hear the same thing:

"It's so nice to finally meet you, Mrs. Flanders. Your husband talks about you all the time. I feel like I've known you for years!"

But the me they think they know is not the one who wakes up with morning breath or burns dinner to a crisp or leaves clothes in the washer so long they sour or has to hire a repairman to tell her the reason the icemaker isn't working is because somebody turned it off.

Not even close. My husband's colleagues are only familiar with the Wonder Woman version of me—the one who runs marathons and writes books and tutors calculus and sings like an angel and never sleeps.

Which would explain why so many of them make an elaborate gesture of obeisance before repeating in detail the most memorable story my husband has told them to date.

I'll admit, his stories do sound pretty incredible. In fact, if I weren't so intimately acquainted with all my balancing foibles, I'd probably feel a little intimidated by my own reputation.

> "Your reputation is in the hands of others. That's what the reputation is. You can't control that. The only thing you can control is your character."
>
> - Wayne W. Dyer

Keep in mind that very few of these people know me except through what my spouse has told them. If he were inclined to focus on the negative instead of on the positive, their perception of me might be radically skewed (and their esteem for him would probably plummet, as well).

So my question is this: How does your husband's reputation fare among your friends? When you are out with the girls or gabbing with coworkers, do you build him up or run him down? What you say reflects on you as much as it does him.

*134*

# Chapter 22 - Guard His Reputation

The Bible tells us, *"An excellent wife is the crown of her husband, but she who shames him is like rottenness in his bones."* (Proverbs 12:4)

Your husband is at your mercy. You know him more intimately than anybody else on the planet. How will you use that knowledge? Will you choose to be a crown or a curse to him?

*"Death and life are in the power of the tongue,"* Scripture warns us. *"He who finds a wife finds a good thing and obtains favor from the LORD."* (Proverbs 18:21-22)

Fitting, the juxtaposition of those two verses, don't you think? Part of what makes a woman a good wife and a crown to her husband is her ability to measure her words, to guard her tongue, to let it be governed by the law of kindness, and to use it to speak words of life:

> "A reputation once broken may possibly be repaired, but the world will always keep their eyes on the spot where the crack was."
>
> - Joseph Hall

- *"Those who guard their mouths and their tongues keep themselves from calamity."* (Proverbs 21:23)
- *"Do not let any unwholesome talk come out of your mouths, but only what is helpful for building others up according to their needs, that it may benefit those who listen."* (Ephesians 4:29)

- *"When there are many words, transgression is unavoidable, But he who restrains his lips is wise."* (Proverbs 10:19)
- *"Those who guard their lips preserve their lives, but those who speak rashly will come to ruin."* (Proverbs 13:3)

Whether or not you appreciate the fact, your husband's reputation is of paramount importance to him.

> "A good name is more desirable than great riches; to be esteemed is better than silver or gold."
>
> - Proverbs 22:1 (NIV)

Most guys say they'd rather feel unloved than disrespected.[1] For ages, men have even fought duels for the sake of their honor. They'd sooner suffer death than have their name besmirched.

Literature, too, is replete with passages extolling the worth of a good reputation. Shakespeare writes in *Othello*:

> "Good name in man and woman...
> Is the immediate jewel of their souls:
> Who steals my purse steals trash...
> But he that filches from me my good name
> Robs me of that which not enriches him,
> And makes me poor indeed."[2]

These lines echo the words of Socrates from two thousand years earlier:

> "Regard your good name as the richest jewel you can possibly be possessed of—for credit is like

fire; when once you have kindled it you may easily preserve it, but if you once extinguish it, you will find it an arduous task to rekindle it again. The way to a good reputation is to endeavor to be what you desire to appear."

And in his magnificent tale of redemption, *Les Misérables,* Victor Hugo made this observation:

> "Whether true or false, *what is said* about men often has as much influence on their lives, and particularly on their destinies, as *what they do*."[3]

Your husband's good name is your good name, too (and vice versa), so guard it well. Honor him in the way you speak of him to family and friends. Protect his reputation.

Don't let minor irritations or disagreements at home tempt you to badmouth him in public.

Live in such a way that others will have no trouble understanding why your husband married you in the first place.

> "Treat a man as if he had a fine reputation to protect, and he will usually endeavor to deserve it."
>
> - Orson Scott Card

## Put It into Practice:

✍ If you were to meet a new group of friends who asked you to tell them something about your husband, what would you say? Think through a few personal anecdotes that illustrate his most admirable qualities, and then next time you're given the opportunity, you'll know just how to answer!

✍ Sometimes a spouse's weakness is just a distorted manifestation of a related strength. My husband, for example, is a bit prone to making impulse purchases, but he is also very quick to help those in need. So if I were going to speak to the way he handles money, rather than grouse about some frivolous thing he's bought, I would focus on the fact that my husband is the most generous man I've ever met. God loves a cheerful giver; should I do less?

✍ If you find yourself among friends who take pleasure in speaking derisively about their husbands, then gently encourage them to change their tunes. If they persist, then limit the time you spend with them or find new friends altogether.[4]

Forgive His
Shortcomings

## Chapter 23

Have you ever met a person who steadfastly refuses to forgive?

I have, and I can tell you, it is not a pretty sight. Hardened jaw, hateful glare—outward beauty is fleeting under the best of circumstances, but it flees much faster when coupled with an impoverished, unforgiving spirit.

Bitterness, when given room to grow, will eat away at your soul like a cancer, compromising your health, your mental acuity, and your interpersonal relationships. When harbored against your spouse, a grudge will slowly suck the life out of your marriage. Left unchecked, it will destroy your love, your joy, your

*139*

peace, and will ultimately leave your home and family in shambles.

To keep this from happening, we must learn to extend forgiveness—not because our spouse deserves it (any more than we do), nor even because he has necessarily requested it, but because God has commanded us to do so:

> *"But when you are praying, first forgive anyone you are holding a grudge against, so that your Father in heaven will forgive your sins, too."* (Mark 11:25, NLT)

One of his disciples once asked Jesus, "How many times shall I forgive my brother when he sins against me? Up to seven times?"

Jesus answered, "Not seven times, but seventy times seven times." He then told the story of a servant who owed his master an exorbitant sum of money he could never hope to repay.[1]

> "A life lived without forgiveness is a prison."
>
> - William Arthur Ward

Rather than selling him (and his wife and children, as well) to recoup the loss, the master took pity on the poor slave and forgave him the enormous debt he owed.

Afterwards, this newly debt-free servant encountered a fellow who owed him pittance. Demanding that the small sum be repaid immediately, the forgiven slave beat his indebted friend mercilessly and then threw him into prison until he should pay his debt in full.

## Chapter 23 - Forgive His Shortcomings

How often are we guilty of the same disparity in our marriages? God has forgiven the enormous debt of our sin against Him, but we want to make our husbands suffer for the smallest of slights against us.

This is neither the formula for a successful marriage nor the path to a fulfilling life. Rather, "A happy marriage," in the words of Ruth Bell Graham, "is the union of two good forgivers."

So please do not hold grudges against your husband. Let go of any bitterness or resentment over wrongs, real or imagined. No marriage can thrive in a hostile environment of judgment and constant criticism, so forgive your husband freely, just as Christ has forgiven you.

> "Forgiveness is not an occasional act, it is a constant attitude."
>
> - Martin Luther King, Jr.

Your husband *will* fall short; he is only human. But don't use that as an excuse to mistreat him. You must forgive and keep forgiving; you must love and keep loving; you must respect and keep respecting —for this is what it will take for your marriage to bloom and thrive:

> *Love is patient, love is kind. It does not envy, it does not boast, it is not proud. **It does not dishonor others, it is not self-seeking, it is not easily angered, it keeps no record of wrongs.** Love does not delight in evil but rejoices with the truth. It always protects, always trusts, always*

*hopes, always perseveres. Love never fails.* (1 Corinthians 13:4-8, NIV, *emphasis added*)

Can you imagine how amazing a marriage would be if both spouses stopped brooding over petty offenses and started demonstrating *this* kind of love to one another? If instead of nursing grudges, each selflessly served, protected and built up the other, hearts brimming with mutual respect and admiration? How beautiful would that be?

> "The weak can never forgive. Forgiveness is the attribute of the strong."
>
> - Mahatma Gandhi

That is the kind of marriage that we have been called to: one that reflects God's all-gracious, sacrificial, never-ending, unremitting love for us.

That sort of love, that kind of marriage, really makes the world stop and take notice, but it can never exist apart from forgiveness. Somebody has to be first to forgive. Why not let it be you?

## Put It into Practice:

✍ Next time you catch yourself perseverating about some way your husband has offended you, recently or long past, take a moment to pray for him. And while you are at it, pray for yourself. Confess your reluctance or inability to forgive him, and ask for God's help in doing so.

✍ Even after we've sincerely tried to forgive those who have wronged us, we can still fall prey to feelings of bitterness and resentment. Music is a powerful weapon for driving these away. Next time you are tempted to rehash an old offense, instead of throwing a pity party, break out a hymnal or put on some worship music and begin singing praises to God. And keep singing until you really mean it.

✍ Reading through the Book of Psalms is also a good project for those who struggle in this area. David suffered many wrongs at the hands of those closest him, including King Saul, whom he faithfully served from childhood, and Absalom, the son of his own flesh. Yet David's focus and trust remained fixed on God, which is where ours should lie, as well.

## Chapter 24

My father was one of the friendliest, most gregarious men I've ever met. He loved people. But he also loved a spirited debate. My mother always said Dad would argue with a fencepost.

Mom was decidedly *not* fond of fiery discussions. She has always detested conflict of any sort. Dad would often tease and pick at and try to get a rise out of Mom, but she would not be baited. He may as well have been arguing with that famed fence post for all the success he had at drawing his wife into a fight.

By nature, I tend to take after my father, but by conscious effort, I try to follow my mother's example.

Scripture says it would be better to live in a desert or in the corner of a roof than in a house with a quarrelsome and ill-tempered wife. (Proverbs 21:19; 25:14) My mother's willingness to "abandon a quarrel before it breaks out"[1] made our home a more pleasant and peaceful place to live, not just for my father, but for us children as well.

By her example, my mother also taught me that I don't always have to have the last word; I don't need to drive home my point; I'm under no obligation to convince others I'm right.

Sometimes, in fact, I'm *not* right. And whenever that's the case, I should simply admit I'm wrong,[2] accept the blame, and be the first to say, "I'm sorry."

It takes two to argue. Isn't it liberating to know that? It takes *two*— and you don't have to be one of them.

"To keep your marriage brimming, With love in the wedding cup, Whenever you're wrong, admit it; Whenever you're right, shut up."[1]

- Ogden Nash

Of course, you may not always see eye-to-eye with your husband. When there are areas of disagreement or concerns that need to be discussed, take care to do so in a calm, cool, collected, and consistently respectful way.

# Chapter 24 - Don't Argue

Communicating respect to your husband does not necessitate keeping all your thoughts to yourself. It does not mean going along with his every whim, even when serious reservations exist. Showing respect is not about suppressing your feelings; it's really more about the tone with which those feelings are expressed.

A disrespectful tone communicates, "Listen, you idiot, let me set you straight on this matter, because it's obvious you don't know what you're talking about."

> "Always and never are two words you should always remember never to use."
>
> - Wendell Johnson

Of course, we would (hopefully) never actually say such a thing, but our husbands will sometimes hear these words in our tone, even when we don't utter them outright.

A respectful tone, by contrast, first hears the other person out. It always gives thoughtful consideration to what is being said, even if the speaker isn't able to articulate his ideas as easily as you yourself might be able to do so. A respectful tone validates the other person by saying, "I see your point," before continuing, "but have you considered...?"

If you are married to a man who deflates anytime you disagree with him, then be especially careful to (1) build him up in every way you can, as he likely struggles with a lack of confidence and/or other insecurities, and (2) pick your battles. Many times, our husbands do things in a different way than we would do them, but that doesn't mean their way is wrong. Go with the flow for as long as possible, then when an issue arises that you really feel strongly about, you will have stored up some goodwill by not having contradicted the two or three dozen choices he's made prior to the current one. It is easy for our husbands to grow weary and lose patience when we argue and second-guess each and every decision they make.

As for preventing difficult discussions from escalating into angry arguments, follow these guidelines to keep tempers from flaring:

1. **Practice Attentive Listening**

   Pay attention to what your spouse is trying to say to you. Hear him out. Don't just pretend to be listening while you mentally rehearse what you plan to say next.

   *"Spouting off before listening to the facts is both shameful and foolish."* (Proverbs 18:13, NLT)

2. **Demonstrate Genuine Love**

   If you will focus on all the reasons you love this person instead of on the things that irritate you about him, you will be much less likely to say something you later regret.

   *"Hatred stirs up conflict, but love covers over all wrongs."* (Proverbs 10:12, NIV)

3. **Maintain Calm Voices**

   Don't allow the pitch to creep up in your conversation. Maintain a gracious, soft-spoken demeanor at all times.

   *"A gentle answer turns away wrath, but a harsh word stirs up anger."* (Proverbs 15:1)

148

4. **Use Word Pictures**

Well thought-out word pictures and analogies are a great way to communicate a concern without being abrasive and accusatory.

*"A word fitly spoken is like apples of gold in pictures of silver."* (Proverbs 25:11, KJV)

5. **Keep Sweet Speech**

Let your words be filled with kindness and seasoned with grace; do not resort to name calling or exaggerated accusations.

*"Sweetness of speech increases persuasiveness."* (Proverbs 16:21)

6. **Exercise Patient Understanding**

Try to see the situation from your spouse's point of view. Be empathetic. Put yourself in his shoes to better appreciate his perspective.

*"Whoever is patient has great understanding, but one who is quick-tempered displays folly."* (Proverbs 14:29, NIV)

7. **Remain Cool-Headed**

Weigh your words carefully, always and only speaking the truth in love. Don't be rash.

*"A hot-tempered person stirs up strife, but the slow to anger calms a dispute."* (Proverbs 15:18)

8. **Show Sincere Humility**

Rid your tone (and your heart) of all pride and condescension, neither of which serve any purpose but to stir up strife and discord.

*"God is opposed to the proud, but gives grace to the humble."* (James 4:6)

## 9. Express Earnest Repentance

Show appropriate, unfeigned remorse over any wrongdoing. Apologize for offensive things you have said or done without excusing your actions or casting blame on your spouse.

*"Those whom I love, I rebuke and discipline. So be earnest and repent."* (Revelation 3:19, NIV)

## Put It into Practice:

✍ Memorize Proverbs 17:14 and endeavor to live by it: "The beginning of strife is like letting out water, So abandon the quarrel before it breaks out."

✍ It may be necessary for you and your husband to agree to disagree on certain topics. Politics is a common example. I know a couple where one spouse is a dyed-in-the-wool conservative and the other is a flaming liberal. They realized long ago that neither was going to change the other's views; nevertheless, they've remained committed to their marriage, as well as to canceling out each other's votes at every election.

✍ Avoid discussing anything while tempers are hot. Bite your tongue until things cool down, then come back to the table once you've both had time to think and pray about the matter at hand.

Follow
His Lead

# Chapter 25

The principle of Biblical submission gets a bad rap in modern times, but it isn't as defunct a concept as its opponents would have us believe. Even militant feminists who chafe at the thought of submitting to a husband routinely submit to *somebody*. Everyone does.

When your boss asks you to file a report or prepare a presentation or contact a client or update an account, and you do so, *that's* submission.

When your literature professor says you must write a 2000-word paper to pass his course, and you turn in the assignment, *that's* submission.

When your commanding officer orders you to fall in line or stand at attention or march in double-time, and you obey without hesitation, *that's* submission.

When the coach tells you to run laps or work on your lay-ups or practice your free throws, and you hit the gym, *that's* submission.

When your conductor taps his baton on the lectern to cue the strings, and you raise the bow to your violin, *that's* submission.

> "In periods where there is no leadership, society stands still. Progress occurs when courageous, skillful leaders seize the opportunity to change things for the better."
>
> - Harry S. Truman

When a state trooper tails you with lights flashing and sirens blaring, and you pull over, *that's* submission.

Submission is not about equality or intelligence or abilities or worth; it is about authority and practicality and responsibility and structure.

If it weren't for submission, if it weren't for our willingness to subject ourselves to a governing authority in order to achieve a higher goal, society would cease to function. We'd have nothing but anarchy and chaos. Any semblance of law and order would be wiped completely away.

The same is true for a family. When Mom and Dad are at odds with one another and the kids refuse to listen or obey, things can get chaotic pretty fast. This is one reason so many homes are falling apart today: families have abandoned God's design for how it all should work.

God commands wives to respect their husbands, husbands to love their wives, and children to obey their parents.[1] He calls men to lead their families with integrity, patience, understanding, and self-sacrifice.[2]

But men who lead need families who follow. Your husband will never be able to fulfill his God-given responsibility to give guidance and direction to his loved ones, if his loved ones refuse to cooperate.

> "A leader takes people where they want to go. A great leader takes people where they don't necessarily want to go, but ought to be."
>
> - Rosalynn Carter

Think of your husband as you'd think of the quarterback on a football team. He can't win the game by himself. He needs other players to take the field with him. Specifically, he needs his teammates on the field—teammates who'll carry out the plays he's calling.

A quarterback is not autonomous. He must answer to the coach, just as a husband must answer to God. If you disagree with the plays he's running, the right response is to approach him apart from the team, during a time-out. If he refuses to listen, you can speak privately to the coach. But don't try to usurp his position. Putting two quarterbacks from the same team on the same field at the same time to simultaneously run different plays—that just won't work. It's bad strategy. It will never result in victory. Besides that, it's confusing for everybody involved.

Likewise, when a wife insists on calling all the shots for her family, she confuses her kids, castrates her husband, and violates the clear command of Scripture:

- *"Wives, submit yourselves to your husbands, as is fitting in the Lord."* (Colossians 3:18)
- *"Wives, submit to your husbands as to the Lord. For the husband is the head of the wife as Christ is the head of the church, His body, of which He is the Savior. Now as the church submits to Christ, so also wives should submit to their husbands in everything."* (Ephesians 5:22-24, NIV)

> "A leader is like a shepherd. He stays behind the flock, letting the most nimble go out ahead, whereupon the others follow, not realizing that all along they are being directed from behind."
>
> - Nelson Mandela

Neither a body nor a family can function well with two heads. So learn to defer to your husband's wishes and let final decisions rest with him.[3] Treat him with deference and respect and understanding, because that is what God requires of you, and by doing this, you honor Him.

156

## Put It into Practice:

✍ No matter what kind of strife or struggles you're facing in your marriage, resist the temptation to view your husband as your adversary. You have an enemy, to be sure, but that enemy is not the man you married. You should be fighting alongside your husband, not against him.

✍ Many husbands do not care to make all the minute-by-minute decisions required to keep a household running smoothly. My own husband, for instance, does not have a strong opinion about whether I put pecans or walnuts in the brownies, or paint our bedroom blue or green, or use Saxon or Bob Jones to teach our kids math, or dress the baby in cotton or synthetics, or plant periwinkles or impatiens in our flowerbed. Many of these choices he delegates to me. If your husband asks you to take care of the decision making in a certain area of your home life, do so to the very best of your ability. This, too, is following his lead.

✍ Some wives hesitate to follow their husband's lead because they are afraid of the direction their husband may take. I understand that concern, but it does not abrogate our responsibility. God alone can change your husband's heart, but He may be waiting to do that until you let Him change yours.

Live the
Respect

## Afterward

"But shouldn't all these things go both ways?"

I hear this question from a lot of readers. Sadly, many wives seem determined not to show an ounce of respect to their spouse, until their spouse starts toeing the same line. "My husband can do all this nonsense for me," they insist, "if he expects any of it in return."[1]

Unfortunately, these women may be waiting a long while—especially if they're married to men as stubborn as themselves.

Somebody has to make the first move.

159

Other wives get it. They understand respect begets respect just as certainly as selfishness begets selfishness. They know they'll reap what they sow.[2]

Do you long for a joyful marriage, a peaceful home, a deeply satisfying relationship with your spouse? Then you must not grow weary in doing good, for you, too, will reap in due season, if you don't lose heart.[3]

"I seriously offend like half of these things," one reader wrote to confess, "so what do I do to change it? I have no idea where to even begin, but I would like to be different so that I can have a peace of mind."

Does this describe you? You're ready to make changes—even radical changes, if need be—but you don't really know where to start.

Well, if your relationship is such that you can talk openly to your husband about this matter, I suggest that you begin there. Let him know you realize there is a problem and are committed to change. Have him browse the contents of this book, ask which areas he thinks you should tackle first, and request that he hold you accountable with a gentle reminder when you revert back to your old habits (which will undoubtedly happen—at least until you're able to establish new ones).

If communication with your husband is not so good at present, then prayerfully consider which areas are most in need of improvement, make a checklist of

> "Courage doesn't always roar.
> Sometimes courage is the quiet voice at the end of the day saying, "I will try again tomorrow."
>
> - Mary Anne Radmacher

the ones you are going to concentrate on first (maybe just pick two or three at a time for starters), write out a plan as to how you hope to accomplish these, and record your progress each day.

For things like kissing your husband goodbye, your written plan might read: "Get up before time for him to leave, brush my teeth so my breath is fresh, walk him to the door when he's ready to go, tell him I hope he has a great day, and plant one on him before he leaves for work." Once it's done, you can check that one off for the day, then forget about it until it's time to do it again tomorrow.

Do the same for all quantifiable goals like praying for your husband, complimenting him, dressing to please him, and cooking meals he likes, etc. List them in a column on a piece of graph paper, put S M T W T F S or write individual dates across the top, and check off each item daily just as soon as it is done. Those are the easy ones.

For indiscrete goals like honoring your husband's wishes, remaining joyful and content, and not nagging, arguing, or complaining, add these items to your list, too, and do your best, by God's grace, to establish new habits in each area of struggle. But don't check off any of these boxes until bedtime, then think back over the

| Goal: | M | T | W | T | F |
|---|---|---|---|---|---|
| Kiss hubby bye | ✓ | ✓ | ✓ | ✓ | ✓ |
| Dress to please | ✓ | ✓ | ✓ | ✓ | ✓ |
| Cook yummy food | ✓ | ✓ | ✓ | ✓ | |
| No nagging | | | ✓ | ✓ | ✓ |
| No arguing | ✓ | ✓ | | | ✓ |
| No excuses | ✓ | ✓ | ✓ | ✓ | ✓ |

day. Did you remain joyful? Check it off and thank God for a day of victory in that area. Did you complain bitterly when your husband did something you didn't like? Then leave the box by "don't complain" blank for today, and try to do better tomorrow.

Think through whatever situation caused you to stumble and map out a plan—in your mind if not on paper—of how you should have responded and the precise steps you will take next time you are faced with the same trigger to ensure that you react in the desired way.[4]

Keep working on these things—not just because you want to improve your marriage, but because you know it's the right thing to do.

"I like this," one reader confided in me. "I can't force my husband to behave how I want him to (and there's NO way he'll go reading a blog looking for suggestions), so I really only have control over myself. I figure if I'm smiling, joyful, and affectionate and give a rip about myself, my house, and my family as you've so controversially suggested, it just might be a win/win."

She's right. So keep plugging away and don't allow yourself to become discouraged. Chances are, your husband will notice and reciprocate in kind. Yet even if that doesn't happen as soon as you think it should, you'll have the satisfaction of knowing that you are doing the right thing.

We are told in Proverbs 18:22 that *"he who finds a wife finds a good thing and obtains favor from the Lord."* Do these twenty-five things consistently, and your life will shine as a testimony to the truth of that verse, whether your husband ever acknowledges that fact or not.

But I'm betting he will.

For Further
Study

# Recommended Reading

The goal of being an excellent wife and building a strong, happy home is one that every married woman should pursue as long as there is life within her. It's a challenge that must be attacked with tireless determination.

As much as I'd like to tell you that, once you get past the first fifteen or twenty or twenty-five years of marriage, you'll be able to prop up your feet and coast the rest of the way, such has not been my experience. Nor have I met any older wives who've indicated it's all smooth sailing after forty or fifty or sixty years, either.

163

One thing you can do to invest in your marriage is to read (and implement!) wise counsel from marriage-building resources, such as the personal favorites I've listed here:

## Books:

*5 Love Languages* (Gary Chapman)
*Created to Be His Help Meet* (Debi Pearl)
*For Better or Best* (Gary Smalley)
*For Women Only* (Shaunti Feldhahn)
*Love and Respect* (Emerson Eggerichs)
*Love for a Lifetime* (James Dobson)
*Love Your Husband/ Love Yourself* (Jennifer Flanders)
*Marriage Builder* (Larry Crabb)
*The Proper Care and Feeding of Husbands* (Laura Schlessinger)

## Websites:

Above Rubies (Nancy Campbell)—
     *http://aboverubies.org/*
Club 31 Women (Lisa Jacobson)—
     *http://club31women.com/*
Focus on the Family (Jim Daly, president)—
     *http://www.focusonthefamily.com/*
For the Family (Pat and Ruth Schwenk)—
     *http://forthefamily.org/*
Loving Life at Home (this one's mine)—
     *http://lovinglifeathome.com/*
The Time-WarpWife (DarleneSchacht)—
     *http://time-warp-wife.blogspot.com/*
To Love, Honor and Vacuum (Sheila Wray Gregoire)
     *http://tolovehonorandvacuum.com/*

My
Sincere Thanks

## Acknowledgements

In the writing of any book, more goes into it than the simple setting of words on a page. There's also a lot of thinking, discussing, developing, and exchanging of viewpoints and ideas. There's the necessary formatting, proofreading, and printing of the message. And there's everyday life with all its needs and responsibilities demanding attention, even in the midst of book writing.

I owe a debt of gratitude to my *Loving Life at Home* readers. Even today, that original "25 Ways" post continues to bring more traffic to my blog than any other post I've ever written. This tells me that communicating respect is an issue women care about. I appreciate the many comments the post received, both from those who agreed with what I'd written and those who didn't. The resultant dialogue helped me to better define, clarify, and support my position for the little volume you now hold in your hands.

To all the precious, like-minded friends God has placed in my life—Janet Baber, Theresa Nicholson, Jacqueline Goode, and all my sweet sisters from FFBC—thank you for your moral support. You bless me.

To my dear mother and lifelong editor, I appreciate your continued attention to detail. Thanks for proofing a digital copy of this book to help me meet my deadlines, even though you'd rather read a hard copy.

To all my children, thank you for being such wonderful people. I've tried to put a bit of each of you into these pages, including Jonathan's positivity, Beth's transparency, David's self-discipline, Samuel's humility, Ben's steadfast encouragement, Joseph's resourcefulness, Rebekah's creativity, Rachel's persistence, Isaac's energy, Daniel's enthusiasm, Gabriel's gentleness, and Abigail's vibrant joy for living. I cannot imagine life without every single one of you. It's an honor and a privilege to be your mother.

To Doug, I was wonderstruck the day I met you, and that feeling has only intensified in the intervening years. I am so glad that you picked me, pursued me, and proposed marriage to me. Agreeing to be your wife was one of the best decisions I've ever made, and I praise God daily for bringing us together. You have my utmost respect. Thanks for working so hard to earn it.

*Soli Deo Gloria,*
Jennifer Flanders

# - Endnotes -

INTRODUCTION: SHOW SOME RESPECT
1.  Please note that this book is not entitled "25 Things Every
    Husband Should Demand from his Wife." (If the guys want a
    list, they should check out my husband's "25 Ways to Express
    Love to Your Wife.")

CHAPTER 1: CHOOSE JOY
1.  Prager, D. *Happiness is a Serious Problem,* pp. 3-4.
    (I don't agree with everything Prager has written in this book,
    but I think he's spot on with this suggestion.)

CHAPTER 4: DON'T INTERRUPT
1.  Brizendine, L. *The Female Brain*, p. 14.

CHAPTER 5: EMPHASIZE HIS GOOD POINTS
1.  Elizabeth Elliot, in a personal letter to the author, dated
    September 30, 1986.
2.  I've seen this anonymous quote attributed to various sources,
    including John F Kennedy (http://quotes-lover.com/quotation
    persons-are-judged-to-be-great-because-of-the-positive-
    qualities-they-posess-not-because-of-the-absence-of-faults) and
    Rita Mae Brown (http://www.worldofquotes.com/quote/5499/
    index.html), but I was unable to verify either of those
    attributions or to track down the original speaker.

CHAPTER 6: PRAY FOR HIM
1.  This is a paraphrase of a quote by Gordon Hinckly: "Get on
    your knees and pray, then get on your feet and work."

# Endnotes

(http://www.goodreads.com/quotes/55592-get-on-your-knees-and-pray-then-get-on-your?auto_login_attempted=true).

## CHAPTER 7: DON'T NAG
1. My husband often says, "You're so sweet," even when I'm not nagging and insists he has always meant it sincerely. Indeed, there's never been even a hint of sarcasm in his tone, but the statement still makes me pause for a moment of self-examination: *Am I really being sweet? Or am I being a little bossy?*
2. God's Word translation of Judges 16:16.

## CHAPTER 9: SMILE AT HIM
1. Flanders, J. *Love Your Husband/ Love Yourself,* p. 83.
2. Charnetski, C. *Feeling Good is Good for You,* p. 83.
3. Gladwell, M. *Blink,* p. 208.
4. I've seen this quote attributed to Stanley Gordon West (author of *Growing an Inch),* but I don't believe it was original with him. The saying is often followed by, "Cry, and you cry alone," but my favorite ending is "Frown, and you're on your own." This is what we tell our children—because nobody likes to be around a pouter or a whiner.
5. Smalley, G. *For Better or for Best,* p. 95.

## CHAPTER 10: RESPOND PHYSICALLY
1. Brizendine, L. *The Female Brain*, p. 71.
2. Flanders, J. *Love Your Husband/ Love Yourself*, pp. 18-19.
3. Charnetski, C. *Feeling Good Is Good For You*, p. 66.
4. Flanders, J. *Love Your Husband/ Love Yourself*, pp. 58-60.
5. *Ibid,* pp. 70-71.
6. Charnetski, C. *Feeling Good Is Good For You*, p. 112.
7. Flanders, J. *Love Your Husband/ Love Yourself*, pp. 94-98.
8. *Ibid,* pp. 103-107.
9. Nelson, T. *Better Love Now*, p. 176-177.
10. Flanders, J. *Love Your Husband/ Love Yourself*, pp. 145-152.
11. This comment, from a girl who identified herself as Essen, was actually made in response to a negative review of a post I wrote called, "Don't Waste Your Girl Power." (You may read my original post here: http://lovinglifeathome.com/2013/07/07/girl-power-dont-waste-it/) Mamamia Rogue editor Rosie Waterland

published her thoughts about my post in a snarky online article entitled, "This Confused Stepford Wife Wants YOU to Have More Sex. For Feminism." (http://www.mamamia.com.au/rogue/girl-power-jennifer-flanders/) Interestingly, I do not think Rosie got the amens she was expecting. Essen's was just one of many responses that defended my position, despite the fact most of the readers' belief systems and life choices look very different from mine.

12. In no way does a wife's chronic disinterest in sex justify a husband's sinful decision to seek it elsewhere, but it does make him considerably more vulnerable to temptation. I believe an unfaithful husband is 100% responsible for his wrong choices and deplorable behavior, but I also believe that a wife bears 100% responsibility for her own actions/reactions toward the man she married. Neither is an island, and—like it or not—what each spouse does affects the other, for good or for bad.

## CHAPTER 11: EYES ONLY FOR HIM
1. Gary Smalley discusses this concept of "lighting up" at length in his book, *For Better or for Best* (see pp. 112-113).

## CHAPTER 12: KISS HIM GOODBYE
1. Hall, Daryl and John Oates in "Kiss on My List" (1981).
2. Flanders, J. *Love Your Husband/ Love Yourself*, p. 88.
3. Demirjian, A. *Kissing*, pp. 177-181.

## CHAPTER 13: FEED HIM HIS FAVORITES
1. Kindlon, D. *Too Much of a Good Thing*, pp. 91, 99, 177, 213.

## CHAPTER 14: CHERISH TOGETHERNESS
1. Eggerichs, E. *Love and Repect*, pp. 240-241.

## CHAPTER 15: DON'T COMPLAIN
1. It was not even so much what they said as how they said it. A wife should never allow derision and contempt to creep into her tone when speaking of her husband.
2. Close, but no cigar.
3. Jesus spelled out our standard in the Sermon on the Mount: "Do unto others as you would have them do unto you." (Luke 6:31) Confucius taught a similar principle: "Never impose on

others what you would not choose for yourself." As did Buddha: "What is hateful to you, don't do to others; what is delightful to you, do for others, too." And Muhammad: "Seek for mankind that of which you are desirous for yourself." In fact, every major religion promotes some version of The Golden Rule. In marriage it boils down to this: "Treat your spouse the way you wish to be treated." For more of my thoughts on this, see my blog post: http://loving lifeathome.com/2013/02/28/the-1-rule-for-building-a-happy-marriage/.

4. This prayer—commonly known as the Serenity Prayer—was originally penned by the American theologian Reinhold Niebuhr (1892–1971).

## CHAPTER 16: RESIST THE URGE TO CORRECT

1. I don't think my husband and I were even married yet when I first made this faux pas. We were at First Baptist Church of Dallas, and Doug made some sort of small-talk comment to a man sharing our elevator, which I immediately and obliviously contradicted. I do not remember anything about that initial conversation, but I'll never forget the look of shock and humiliation in my beloved's eyes when he pulled me aside afterwards and whispered, "*Please,* don't ever do that to me again"—a reasonable request I've done my best to honor ever since.

2. This is a purely hypothetical example. My husband is not an avid fisherman. In fact, I once spotted a plaque at Hobby Lobby that perfectly captured his feelings about the sport. It read: "Life is too short to go fishing...." Knowing Doug would wholeheartedly agree with that sentiment, I thought fleetingly of buying the plaque for him, when I noticed the other half of the quote. The message on the sign actually read, "Life is too short to go fishing only on the weekend!" Ha! Needless to say, I didn't bring it home, but we did have a good laugh about it that evening.

3. This is but another hypothetical example. I'm the one in our family who has trouble remembering right from left, not my husband.

4. Experience talking here.

# Endnotes

5. He also hates coconut, which is just weird. And he skips shaving whenever he's on vacation—something I used to take as a personal insult (silly me), but have since learned to understand and accept. Besides, his beard looks much more distinguished (and not so much like a terrorist) now that he has a little gray in it.

6. I made a wise choice: "Researchers have found that moms who are the least critical of their husbands and encourage the dad's interactions with the child fare best when it comes to staying together," writes Louann Brizendine in *The Male Brain*, "[and have also] shown that the [physical and boisterous] way fathers play with their children makes their kids more curious and improves their ability to learn." (p. 88)

## CHAPTER 17: DRESS TO PLEASE HIM

1. After breastfeeding nearly continuously for twenty-five years, I've also discovered that long hair is handy for hiding milk leaks—just toss it in front of your shoulder, and no one need ever know.

2. A reader by the name of K. Boyd expounded upon this point in the comment section of my blog. She made the following very astute observation: *"It doesn't seem to offend women that every magazine in every grocery check stand in America [tells you how to dress] to impress that guy at the office, how to have amazing sexual experiences, what's the latest makeup trend, etc. Why isn't that demeaning? They are pimping you out to men who don't care about you or the state of your heart when you wear those cute clothes [or] use those makeup tips [or] follow all of those suggestions for amazing sex, and then the guy never calls you back. Why is it so archaic to be willing to do everything you possibly can to show love and care, passion and compassion to the person you have vowed to love and cherish all the days of your life, until death do you part?"*

3. Schlessinger, L. *The Proper Care and Feeding of Husbands*, p. 121.

## CHAPTER 18: KEEP THE HOUSE TIDY

1. Unless, of course, you live in a house with one or more small children who neither share their parents' yearning for order nor appreciate the fact that shoes belong on assigned shelves in the

# Endnotes

garage, *not* hidden in the toy chest, kicked under a bed, buried in the sandbox, or stuck inside the legs of an inside-out pair of blue jeans in the bottom of the laundry hamper.

## CHAPTER 19: BE CONTENT
1.  Carnegie, D. *How to Win Friends and Influence People.*

## CHAPTER 20: TAKE HIS ADVICE
1.  Dr. Louann Brizendine has written a book entitled *The Male Brain* entirely devoted to this topic. It is a fascinating read, and I highly recommend it to anyone desiring a better understanding of the men and boys in their lives. The chapter on "The Daddy Brain" alone is worth the price of the book.
2.  Brizendine, L. *The Male Brain*, pp. 97-100.
3.  *Ibid,* p. 96.

## CHAPTER 22: GUARD HIS REPUTATION
1.  Feldhahn, S. *For Women Only*, p. 23. According to Feldhahn's surveys, 74% of men would choose to feel "alone and unloved" rather than "inadequate and disrespected."
2.  Shakespeare, W. *Othello*, III, iii, 154-161.
3.  Hugo, V. *Les Misérables*, p. 1. (*emphasis added*)
4.  I am not suggesting you turn your back on a friend who has come to you privately and sincerely seeking prayer and counsel for a specific problem in her marriage. This situation is entirely different than the one I described, where wives are merely complaining for the sake of complaining and have no real desire to better their circumstances or improve their marriage. Rather, they're trying to outdo one another in terms of who has the stupidest spouse and therefore deserves the most sympathy. That sort of behavior is destructive to everybody involved, and you should never willingly be a part of it.

## CHAPTER 23: FORGIVE HIS SHORTCOMINGS
1.  To read the story in its entirety, see Matthew 18:21-35.

## CHAPTER 24: DON'T ARGUE
1.  Actually *saying* "shut up" at our house is strictly verboten, but I've always been a big fan of Ogden Nash, so I'm making an

exception to include that phrase here, as it fits the poem's context and rhymes nicely.

2. My husband once accused me of never being able to admit it when I'm wrong. Unwilling to prove him right on that count, I immediately owned up to my mistake in that original conversation, then actively looked for opportunities in the weeks and months that followed to admit being wrong without his prompting. Not to toot my own horn or anything, but I'm actually quite good at it now. Clearly, then, his original allegation was grossly inaccurate, though I've yet to hear him admit that he was wrong about *that*.

## CHAPTER 25: FOLLOW HIS LEAD

1. Ephesians 5:22-6:4; Colossians 3:18-20.
2. Integrity: Proverbs 20:7.
   Patience: Colossians 3:19.
   Understanding: 1 Peter 3:7.
   Self-Sacrifice: Ephesians 5:25.
3. As much as some wives insist that, in their marriage, all decisions are mutual and there is no leader, this simply cannot be true. Sooner or later there will come a time when husband and wife must make a decision over which they have not been able to agree. At such a time, one of them will make that decision, and the other will abide by it. Even the decision *to postpone a decision* is itself a decision.

## AFTERWORD: LIVE THE RESPECT

1. This particular quote came from a reader who identified herself as Carolina, but it is representative of many such responses I received.
2. Galatians 6:7.
3. Galatians 6:9, paraphrased.
4. This is the most effective way I know to exchange bad habits for good ones. If you are serious about making radical changes in the way you relate to your husband and you like to read, I would highly recommend the bestselling book *The Power of Habit* by Charles Duhigg. It is a broad book (not specifically about marriage, but certainly applicable) that is both fascinating and inspiring.

# - References -

Brizendine, Louann. (2006). *The Female Brain*. New York, NY: Morgan Road Books.

_____. (2010). *The Male Brain.* New York, NY: Broadway Books.

Carnegie, Dale. (1998). *How to Win Friends and Influence People.* New York, NY: Pocket Books.

Charnetski, Carl and Francis Brennan. (2001). *Feeling Good is Good for You: How Pleasure Can Boost Your Immune System and Lengthen Your Life.* USA: Rodale, Incorporated.

Demirjian, Andrea. (2006). *Kissing: Everything You Ever Wanted to Know about One of Life's Sweetest Pleasures.* New York, NY: Perigee Books.

Eggerichs, Emerson. (2004). *Love and Respect: The Love She Most Desires, The Respect He Desperately Needs.* Nashville, TN: Thomas Nelson.

Flanders, Jennifer. (2010). *Love Your Husband/ Love Yourself: Embracing God's Purpose for Passion in Marriage.* Tyler, Texas: Prescott Publishing.

Feldhahn, Shaunti. (2004). *For Women Only: What You Need to Know about the Inner Lives of Men.* Colorado Springs, CO: Multinomah Publishers.

Gladwell, Malcolm. (2005). *Blink: The Power of Thinking Without Thinking.* New York, NY: Little, Brown and Company.

Hugo, Victor. (1987). *Les Misérables:A New Unabridged Translation by Lee Fahnestock and Norman MacAfee.* New York, NY: Signet Classics.

# References

Kindlon, Dan. (2001). *Too Much of a Good Thing: Raising Children of Character in an Indulgent Age.* New York, NY: Hyperion

Nelson, Tommy. (2008). *Better Love Now: Making Your Marriage a Lifelong Love Affair.* Nashville, TN: B&H Publishing Group.

Prager, Dennis. (1998). *Happiness is a Serious Problem: A Human Nature Repair Manual.* New York, NY: Harper.

Schlessinger, Laura. (2004). *The Proper Care and Feeding of Husbands.* New York, NY: HarperCollins Publisher.

Smalley, Gary. (2012). *For Better or for Best: A Valuable Guide to Knowing, Understanding, and Loving Your Husband.* Grand Rapids, MI: Zondervan.

Thanks for taking time to read my book, *25 Ways to Communicate Respect to Your Husband.* I pray that your marriage will be abundantly blessed as you seek to honor your man!

If you would like to read more, I encourage you to visit my family website (*www.flandersfamily.info*), follow my blog (*http://lovinglifeathome.com*), or join me on Facebook (*www.facebook.com/love.your.husband.yourself*).

If you have comments, questions, or other feedback, you may write me at *flandersfamily@flandersfamily.info.* I'm not able to respond to most inquiries personally, but I do read all of my mail and will try to address questions of general interest online.

Blessings,

*Jennifer Flanders*

Don't miss the companion volume to
*25 Ways to Communicate Respect to Your Husband*

# Coming in February 2015

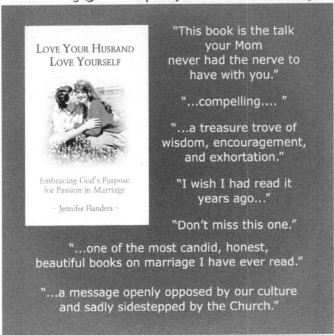

Made in United States
Orlando, FL
08 September 2023

36812279R00114